KNITTING

for

Beginners

A Step-by-Step Guide to Learning Knitting Techniques and Starting Easy to Follow Knitting Projects

By Michelle Welsh

© **Copyright 2020 - All rights reserved.**

The content contained within this book may not be reproduced, duplicated or transmitted without direct written permission from the author or the publisher.

Under no circumstances will any blame or legal responsibility be held against the publisher, or author, for any damages, reparation, or monetary loss due to the information contained within this book. Either directly or indirectly.

Legal Notice:

This book is copyright protected. This book is only for personal use. You cannot amend, distribute, sell, use, quote or paraphrase any part, or the content within this book, without the consent of the author or publisher.

Disclaimer Notice:

Please note the information contained within this document is for educational and entertainment purposes only. All effort has been executed to present accurate, up to date, and reliable, complete information. No warranties of any kind are declared or implied. Readers acknowledge that the author is not engaging in the rendering of legal, financial, medical or professional advice. The content within this book has been derived from various sources. Please consult a licensed professional before attempting any techniques outlined in this book.

By reading this document, the reader agrees that under no circumstances is the author responsible for any losses, direct or indirect, which are incurred as a result of the use of information contained within this document, including, but not limited to, — errors, omissions, or inaccuracies.

KNITTING FOR BEGINNERS

Table of Contents

Introduction vii

Chapter One: The History Of Knitting 1

    Knitting's Earliest History 2

    The Industrial Revolution: Knitting By Machine 4

    The 1900s: A Waning Interest In Knitting 9

    The 21st Century: The Resurrection Of Knitting 14

Chapter Two: Essential Tools 21

    Needles 23

    Yarn 27

    Scissors 28

    Tape Measure 29

    Tapestry Needle 31

    Stitch Markers 32

    Stitch Holders 34

    Row Counter 35

    Needle Gauge 36

    Yarn Bobbins 37

    Yarn Threader 38

    Yarn Guide 39

    Needle Caps 40

Chapter Three: Knitting Patterns 46

    Slip Knot And Casting On 47

    Knit Stitch 51

    Purl Stitch 53

KNITTING FOR BEGINNERS

Stockinette Stitch 56

Garter Stitch 58

Rib Stitching 59

1/1 Rib Stitch 60

2/2 Rib Stitch 62

2/2 Garter Stitch Rib 64

Broken Rib Stitch... 66

Seed Stitch... 67

Moss Stitch... 70

Little Granite Stitch 72

Basket Weave Stitch 75

Chapter Four: Essential Techniques 83

Binding Off (Also Known As Casting Off)................................ 84

Weaving Ends.. 87

Sewing Seams 90

Fixing A Dropped Stitch 95

Fixing Holes 98

Changing Colors 101

Terminology And Abbreviations 104

Chapter Five: Knitting Projects..112

Project #1: A Simple Washcloth... 113

Project #2: A Simple Beanie... 118

Project #3: A Floor Pouf 124

Chapter Six: Common Mistakes To Avoid...........................129

Stopping In The Middle Of A Row 130

v

KNITTING FOR BEGINNERS

    Making Your Stitches Too Tight 131

    Growing Or Shrinking The Size Of Your Rows 133

    Messy Knitting 134

Final Words **137**

INTRODUCTION

Knitting is an art form which has been around since at least the 11th century of the common era, which is our modern era. Knitting is used to create textile products such as blankets, clothes, mittens, pillows and whatever other textiles you can imagine. The technique is incredibly popular and widely known. It used to be exceedingly common for women to be taught knitting in school, though this has largely fallen out of fashion, which is unfortunate. Knitting is an awesome skill. Who wouldn't want to learn how to make their own clothes or pillows? It can save a lot of money, plus it always feels great to receive a present that was handmade by someone. There is so much care and love in such a present. Learning a skill like this can be a money maker depending on the time and energy you are willing to spend, but it can also save you a lot of money over the course of a lifetime. Rather than purchasing an overpriced and low-quality sweater that is just going to be worn out in a couple years, you can knit yourself one that will last a lot longer. Not to mention the simple fact that you made the sweater, so you know exactly how to fix any particular section that starts to degrade and experience wear and tear.

Knitting looks quite a bit like crochet, a similar skill used to create textile artworks. Crochet is done by using a single stick-like object, called a crochet hook, to create interconnected loops of fabric. Knitting is also done by creating interconnected loops but it does so by using two knitting needles to manage the loops. To those who don't know much about these skills, they are easily confused for one another. Both skills are used to create similar objects but there are clear differences between the two, which we will be getting into later.

One of the things that can be difficult about getting into knitting (or crochet for that matter) is the unique vocabulary that has been built around the skill. If you head out and get your hands on a knitting pattern, you'll find that it is filled with abbreviations and terminology that can leave you scratching your head. Many people who begin to learn to knit get to this terminology and give up. In this book, we'll look at this terminology before doing some hands-on projects but we're not going to use confusing abbreviations. Patterns will be written here so that beginners who have never encountered a knitting abbreviation can follow along. This won't be the norm when finding patterns out in the world but it is important to me that you are able to easily follow along. Once you've done a few projects you will have a sense of the flow of a project and it will be much easier to follow along with patterns on your own.

But there is a lot of book to cover before we get there!

KNITTING FOR BEGINNERS

In the first chapter we'll take a look at the history of knitting. When did it start and just how did it go from being widely taught to being selectively learned only by those with an interest in it? These questions and more will get covered in this theory heavy chapter.

Chapter two will instead focus on the tools we use in knitting. Sure, we need yarn and knitting needles but what else? Or maybe I should have asked what kind? You didn't think that there was only one type of knitting needle, did you? Don't worry if you did, I know I certainly did before I learned how to knit!

Chapter three will begin our hands-on training. In this chapter we will look at the common knitting stitch patterns that every beginner should learn. Knitted sweaters will show a lot of variation from sweater to sweater, depending almost entirely on what stitches you decide to use. Of course there are other factors that impact this, such as type of yarn and color, but the stitches will create a different looking texture in the piece.

Chapter four will move on from these essential stitch patterns that beginners need to learn and it will instead focus on those essential techniques that haven't been covered yet. We'll also discuss the terminology of knitting in this chapter, so you can expect to find yourself coming back to reference chapter four from time to time until you are comfortable with the abbreviations and terms you'll find that knitters use.

Chapter five makes up the meat of the book as it is here that we'll turn our attention over to knitting our own amazing projects. These projects have been chosen for the way that they help teach beginners about the various elements of knitting discussed previously. They are like the training wheel version of a project, they'll get you out there and to work on the skill but they won't push you too hard. It is better to start small and increase your skill from project to project than it is to try to complete an extremely difficult project right out the gate. You are far more likely to burn out on knitting if you took this latter approach, which is what we're trying to avoid.

Finally, we come to the last chapter, chapter six. In this chapter we will explore the most common mistakes that new knitters make. It is always frustrating to make a mistake, though they are an important part of learning any skill, and so we will look at the most commonly reported mistakes so that we don't fall into the trap of repeating them ourselves.

The flow of the book can thus be thought of as a history lesson, a shopping list and then lots of hands-on practice to really master the skills. I encourage you to knit along at home, practicing the stitches as they are described and working on the projects in chapter five in order of appearance. You don't have to, of course, as the knowledge in the book will still be extremely valuable to you either way, but the language I use in writing will assume you have been following along at home.

But what are we waiting for? Flip the page and let's dig into this rewarding and fascinating practice!

CHAPTER ONE

THE HISTORY OF KNITTING

Knitting is a technique of textile creation that has a long history. This shouldn't be surprising considering how easy knitting actually is. Learning how to knit takes time, patience and practice, but it is not some esoteric, overly complex amalgamation of art forms. Rather, it is one of the easiest ways we have to create clothing and other useful textiles.

In this chapter we are going to take some time to look into the history of knitting. This topic is fascinating to me, as the history of art always is, yet I think that it provides value beyond simply being interesting. There is a rich history of knitting that reaches back centuries and yet the most intriguing area of this history is the last one hundred years. Knitting has changed a lot in the last century and these changes help explain the surge, fall and resurgence of its popularity within the general population.

Knitting's Earliest History

Knitting is a particularly useful technique of textile creation because of how simple it is. Techniques like weaving may have historical roots that go back far longer than knitting does but knitting is a much more popular technique thanks to the ease of creation. Since knitting doesn't require much equipment, simply some yarn or wool and the knitting needles, it makes for a technique that is highly mobile. Nomadic tribes thus really took to knitting as a form of creation since they could easily transport projects from campsite to campsite.

Yet the oldest extant artifact we have is a part of socks that were knitted in Egypt sometime around the 11th century. This isn't to say that it is the first time that knitting was used historically. It is almost certain that knitting traces its way back much further; one such example that points towards this is similar techniques for textile creation from nearly ten centuries prior to the Egyptian socks. But fabrics aren't known for their longevity and many items created throughout history have since been lost to time and decay. That we found knitted socks in Egypt should be no surprise, the dry weather conditions of the country have done wonders for preserving ancient history. But just how many knitted items have been lost to history is impossible to say.

Many histories of knitting place the origin of the practice in the Middle East and this isn't surprising when you consider that knitted objects first came into Europe through Muslim practitioners from the Iberian peninsula. These Muslim knitters were highly regarded and sought after by the Christian Spanish royals and there are many high-quality knitted items found in the royal tombs throughout the area. One of the oldest is a pair of gloves in the tomb of Prince Fernando de la Cerda. The prince passed away in 1275 and so we can date these items quite accurately. Another early example of a knitted item includes a fragment of a larger item, possibly a mitten, found in Estonia, which dates back to the 13th century.

Knitting began to crop up more frequently from this point forward. There are paintings from the 1300s which show the Virgin Mary knitting, for example. London, Amsterdam, Newcastle, Oslo and other famous European cities had knitted goods listed on their tax lists, with the frequency of reporting increasing so that by the 14th century it is safe to say that knitted items were a part of everyday life. From this point onwards it becomes clear that knitting has been taken up by the Europeans and they began to design their own stitches going forward, leading to much of what we know about knitting today. It would continue to grow in popularity, becoming extremely important to the history of Europe, Scotland, Ireland and the rest of the Western world.

KNITTING FOR BEGINNERS

This form of knitting, as we see from paintings depicting it, is quite traditional. In fact, the knitting we'll be practicing and perfecting in this book shares more of its DNA with this historical knitting than it does with the knitting practices that the Industrial Revolution brought into being. Yet we can't ignore the importance of this Revolution, as it greatly affected knitting as we know it.

The Industrial Revolution: Knitting By Machine

To say that the Industrial Revolution changed the world is the understatement of the century. The Industrial Revolution didn't just change the world, it completely reshaped it. It transformed the world into a new place and it began the transition into the modern world. Modernity certainly didn't happen overnight. The early modern period encompasses this time. This came to an end with the Age of Revolutions and brought us into the late modern period. This period saw the French Revolution, the American Revolution, the industrial revolution and the great divergence. This was a period of time in which everything was getting shaken up and it would last until the postmodern movement that followed the end of World War II in 1945. This was a period in which the world shifted. And so, too, did knitting.

Knitting is most often thought of as being a physical activity in which the knitter uses their hands and arms to guide the knitting needles to create loops to turn into stitches. These stitches are then followed one by another to create beautiful and impressive patterns. We know from our older paintings that knitting was handled in this way. Indeed, the Virgin Mary was shown knitting by hand in Tommaso da Modena's *Our Lady Knitting* (circa 1325-1375), as well as in Buxtehude Altar's 1400-1410 masterpiece *Visit of the Angel*. To look at knitting in the modern world, that is to say today's world that you and I find ourselves living in, we see knitting is still performed most often by hand.

This wasn't the case for knitting during the industrial revolution. William Lee, an Englishman and member of the clergy, invented the stocking frame in 1589. Also called the mechanical knitting machine, the stocking frame was used to create textiles in a method called framework knitting. Lee's machine used a separate needle for each loop in the project, though the design meant it could only be used for straight knitting. The needles were attached to a bar which would push forward. Thread was laid onto the needles which would form loops before being pushed down, forward and then back. This would create evenly spaced loops in a fraction of the time it took to do it by hand.

Looking for a patent for his device, Lee sent Queen Elizabeth I a pair of black stockings but she declined them. They were too coarse for the ankles of royalty, she claimed. Also, in a turn of events that is reflective of the modern fear of automation, the Queen was also worried that Lee's machine would put people out of work. King Henry IV of France had no such worry and, considering how much France and England were at odds in those days, it shouldn't come as any surprise that he eagerly offered to support Lee and his new mechanical knitting machine. Lee moved to France and built a factory. From this first factory came others and this new form of knitting was taken up all across Europe. It was nearly one hundred years later that Lee's invention was adopted in his home of England, though here it was looked at more as a family activity and less as a professional occupation.

Mechanical knitting machines became quite popular in Nottingham, where they were used to create beautiful lace patterns. This was one of the few places that truly embraced the mechanical knitting machine as an industry standard, earning the city and the surrounding area a reputation for their hosiery. This reputation and the widespread use of the mechanical knitting machine in the area continued to grow, though not at an impressive rate. It wasn't until the circular knitting machine was invented that this reputation really took off. This new knitting machine was portable and this made it easier for people to get involved in this style of knitting. Rather than requiring an entire factory for the stocking frame, this new mechanical knitting machine could be used at home and people were also able to rent it out in this manner.

But the adoption of knitting factories wasn't really a thing. Some popped up in pretty much every country in Europe but they were vastly outnumbered by those knitters who stuck with their own two hands to make their wares. It wasn't until the middle of the 1800s that the transition really began to happen in a large way and that was thanks to the invention of the steam-powered knitting machine. These machines were powered through steam and thus they are closer-aligned to our modern factory machines compared to Lee's original design. It was this, the invention of a knitting machine that used some form of non-human power, that caused factories to open up at shockingly fast rates. This in tandem saw a decline in knitting by hand. To knit by hand was no longer a viable option for those looking to earn money. A large swath of the working population had to either transition to working in these knitting factories or they had to find new careers, while those who continued to knit by hand did so primarily as a hobby.

Here we find ourselves coming to the 1900s. The landscape for knitting has changed. It moved into mass production and it wasn't slowing down. Most of the clothes that we wear these days are mass produced. If you purchase pillows, sweaters, blankets, curtains, really pretty much any textile then you are purchasing a machine-made item. It is rare to find items that are made by hand these days, at least when it comes to purchasing in stores. The decline in handmade items greatly informs the following hundred years.

KNITTING FOR BEGINNERS

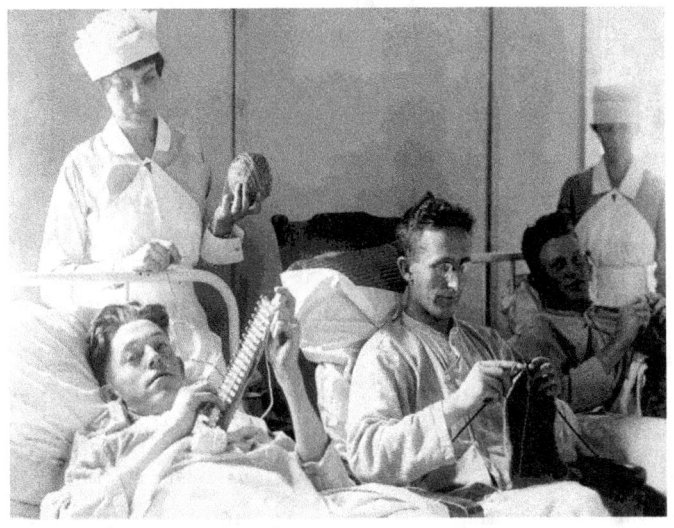

The 1900s: A Waning Interest in Knitting

The majority of knitting was now being done mechanically and so the history of knitting entered into a bit of a dark period, with important elements popping up from time to time, but, generally, fading interest.

One important piece of knitting history was the way knitting interacted with the events of World War I. Citizens came together - men, women and children - to all knit lots and lots of clothing for the Allied soldiers. They would send them socks and hats, sweaters and mittens, anything that could be useful for soldiers who were on the front lines. The war was a notoriously brutal one because it was fought in trenches, with horrible wet and cold conditions. For many soldiers it was these knitted pieces that allowed them to get through without developing hyperthermia. The rise in knitting over these four years actually led to many songs about knitting and magazines reports about the knitting craze that swept the nation. Unfortunately, that did not last once the war ended.

The 1920s saw knitting travel from Russia to China in a manner which was reflective of Europe first discovering the practice those many centuries before. The Russian civil war saw the White Russians; many of them fled to China. China was preparing for its own civil war at the time and so they moved these Russians out to the East. Along this journey the Russians taught the Chinese how to knit. Instead of using yarn, they used the hair of the camels that they were riding. These caravan men then continued the practice of knitting, reaching back to grab a handful of camel hair whenever they ran out. They would knit as they rode, the camels both transporting them and providing them with socks and other warm items at the same time.

Post-World War I Europe saw an increase in knitted fashion. This is likely to do with the fact that so many people had taken up knitting during the war that it was thought of as a new fad. It was in the 1920s that the knitted sweater became a favorite of grandmothers across the globe. Knitting had mostly been used for practical purposes up until then, such as keeping soldiers or fisherman warm. But this decade saw these styles being used by people of all genders, ages and industries. A rise in Fair Isle knitting was seen in this decade, which was a style that the Prince of Wales made popular. The top brass of the fashion world started to wear knitted clothes, too, and Vogue magazine began running patterns in its pages.

It would seem that this period heralded a new love of knitting and the style entered into popular fashions. Yet this short burst of popularity wasn't to last.

The 1930s brought The Great Depression that, in turn, actually increased the amount of knitting that was being done. It was easy to knit, after all, and doing so meant you didn't have to purchase clothes. It was cheaper to purchase yarn and make a piece of clothing. Everyone made sure to save money wherever they could. Both knitting by hand and knitting by machine increased in this decade.

World War II saw a fall in knitting, though at this point knitted clothes were becoming a representation of the hardship of the previous decade and so they were no longer quite as fashionable as they had been in the 1920s. With the war came propaganda that told citizens not to knit new clothing for themselves. If they ripped their socks, they were to patch them up instead of making a whole new pair. The problem was that there wasn't enough wool to go around, the soldiers needed it to stay warm. So instead of purchasing wool and making new items, people were encouraged to take apart old items and reuse that wool instead.

The end of the war did bring another small increase in the popularity of knitting. The 1950s and 1960s saw a rise in knitting thanks to yarn becoming available in more colors than ever before. These new colors brought new designs, new fashions and a rise in knitting. This is the point in which knitting first really begins to be taught in schools in a widespread manner, which in and of itself is actually quite shocking. It was taught as a skill rather than a hobby, but it is an odd skill to teach when we consider that factories were more popular at this point than knitting by hand. It is also shocking because it started to be taught only in the 1950s and 1960s and the biggest decline of interest was a couple decades away.

In the 1980s, knitting was seen as old-fashioned, something to be done away with. Yarn wasn't selling very well. Knitting patterns weren't selling at all. Schools had steadily stopped teaching knitting in school. It just wasn't a popular skill anymore thanks to the fact that the styles seemed out of touch with modern fashion, plus machine knitting was cheaper, easier and quicker than knitting by hand. Why knit yourself a sweater over several weeks when you could purchase one for $10 and wear it the same day?

Fashions at this point started to move away from knitting, so the style wasn't hooking people like it used to, but another important factor was the rise in synthetic fabrics. Many of these fabrics could not be worked by hand. The average person didn't have access to them and so the only way to purchase clothing or textiles made out of these was to go with store-bought goods. These new fabrics and style trends completely wrecked the knitting industry and technological advancements such as computerized knitting machines continued to push the average person even further away from hand knitting.

By the time the 90s came around, there was just no industry for knitting anymore. Most of the companies that made their money in this field had folded and many stores dedicated to selling fabrics and teaching knitting closed their doors. This isn't to say that the practice disappeared completely. There were still speciality publications aimed at the hobbyists and patterns were still being produced, only at an incredibly lower rate than ever before. Yet the 90s also saw the rise in craft fairs that helped bring hobbyists together to forge friendships and teach each other. However, for the most part, it seemed that this practice was set to fade into the past, with each subsequent generation less and less interested in it.

That is… until the invention and widespread adoption of the internet in the early 21st century.

The 21st Century: The Resurrection of Knitting

The internet has changed the world in more ways than we could even begin to imagine. It would take a dozen books the same size as this one to even make a dent in the discussion. But one of the things that we all understand is that the internet has made collaborating with others easier than ever through social media, forums and video sites, like YouTube. We can share our photos, our creations, make videos to teach how they were made and more. And we most certainly make use of them.

This has had a great impact on crafting. As many people began to move away from knitting, there were those that found themselves the only person in their town with an interest. It's hard to share tips and tricks and learn lessons from friends when you don't have any nearby. But the internet has helped connect crafters together. All it takes to make a new knitting friend online is to search the topic on Google and respond to the people you see talking about it. There are tons of websites dedicated to making your own crafts and many of these include sections on knitting, but there are just as many sites that focus exclusively on knitting. The internet and its do-it-yourself culture saved knitting from fading away.

There were other developments within the realm of knitting that have also helped to change the practice. For one, the cost of yarn has dropped significantly. You used to have to acquire fibers from animals (sheep, alpaca, etc.) which made the practice pretty expensive thanks to the time you had to invest in harvesting. Since harvesting has gotten easier, prices have dropped. It is also easier to harvest plant fibers, too, these days. Meanwhile, the flip side of this is that there has also been a rise in expensive, exotic fabrics. People use silk, bamboo and even yak fibers in knitting nowadays. These exotic fabrics have helped destroy the stigma that knitted objects are somehow less impressive or less fashionable than other forms of textiles.

Another thing that has helped to fuel the resurgence in knitting is our celebrity culture. We love celebrities here in North America and so when we see some of our favorite celebrities knitting, it should come as no surprise that pattern and yarn sales go up accordingly. Dakota Fanning, Cameron Diaz and Julia Roberts are just a few of the celebrities that have been known to knit their own projects. However, these are all women, which may reinforce the cultural idea that knitting is somehow a woman's hobby. This attitude doesn't make sense when we look at knitting historically, since men, women and children all knitted historically. Rather it has to do with the fact that knitting was taught to women in schools rather than to men. But celebrities like Carlos Zachrison have helped to show the world that knitting can be a man's hobby.

One of the best things about knitting in this day and age is how easy it is to find patterns. The internet is filled with patterns for amazing items. You want to make a sweater? A quick Google search for "knitting sweater patterns" returns 28,600,000 results. Many of these pages are useless; after all, who goes past the second or third page of Google results? But it does show up just how widespread knitting has become. There are millions of resources, millions of patterns. Thanks to the internet it is safe to say that today is the best time to be a knitter; there are more knitters, more information and more patterns than ever before and all of it is available at your fingertips as long as you know how to use it.

KNITTING FOR BEGINNERS

Speaking of using it, let's turn now to an examination of the tools we use in knitting.

KNITTING FOR BEGINNERS

Chapter Summary

- The oldest knitted artifact we have comes from the 11th century and was discovered in Egypt where the weather is perfect for preserving goods of this type.

- It is thought that knitting comes from the Middle East and was spread through Europe by Muslim practitioners hailing from the Iberian peninsula.

- Knitting spread quickly and paintings from the 1300s even showed the Virgin Mary knitting.

- Knitting changed forever when William Lee, an Englishman who was a member of the clergy, invented the mechanical knitting machine in 1589.

- Lee's machine was looked down upon in his home country of England but the French offered him patronage.

- Within a few centuries knitting transitioned from a thing done primarily by hand to one done mostly in factories.

- World War I saw knitting at home become popular again as citizens knitted clothing and supplies for the troops.

- The Great Depression saw an increase in knitting, as it was cheaper to make your own clothes rather than purchase them.

- World War II saw many people knitting clothing for the troops and there was even propaganda aimed at convincing citizens not to knit for themselves because the troops needed the supplies so badly.

- Knitting became a regularly taught subject in schools during the 1950s and 1960s, but by the 1980s it had all but vanished as clothing prices decreased and new synthetic fabrics became more and more popular.

- Many knitting stores went out of business during the 1980s and 1990s.

- It wasn't until the rise of the internet that knitting began to get popular again, as the internet connected hobbyists from all over the world and let them share tips, advice and patterns with each other.

- Celebrities have also been photographed knitting and this, in turn, led to more people picking up the skill.

In the next chapter you will learn about all the tools you need to start knitting. There aren't that many of them since one of the best parts of knitting is how easy it is to get started. You don't need to spend a lot of money or purchase a lot of esoteric gear.

CHAPTER TWO

ESSENTIAL TOOLS

Knitting is such an amazing skill to learn because it allows you to save a ton of money on clothing and the like, as you make your own textiles. There are many skills which allow you to save money making your own projects but they often require a fairly large initial investment.

Not so with knitting.

Knitting is doubly amazing because it is extremely cheap to get started. You can have a fully functioning knitting kit for less than $50. Of course we must be clear here and realize that we're talking about knitting by hand. Purchasing a knitting machine will be more expensive, but we're not going to concern ourselves with machine knitting in this book. With a skill like this it is always best to learn by hand.

In this chapter we're going to look at the tools necessary for knitting. These include those tools which fit under the essential header such as your needles themselves. But there are also many tools which aren't necessarily essential but which will make your knitting experience a thousand times more enjoyable, such as a row counter or a needle gauge. Consider this chapter your research for a shopping list. Once you've gotten the gear from this chapter, you'll be ready to start practicing your beginner stitches in the next chapter, learning those essential techniques we haven't covered yet in the chapter after that, and then making our first projects in chapter five. But if you don't purchase gear, you'll have a hard time making full use of the information from the next three chapters.

Needles

It would be impossible to get into knitting without purchasing some needles. This shouldn't be a surprise, considering that knitting is a form of textile creation that is distinguished by the way you use two needles to create loops and stitches. They're pretty much as essential to knitting as yarn is.

Yet there are forms of knitting that use neither needles nor yarn. These are much more unique forms of knitting and not at all what is meant when knitting is referenced in conversation or discussed online. So, for our purposes, needles are as important to knitting as breathing is to living.

That doesn't mean that every needle is made the same. There are actually three different types of knitting needles that we find most commonly used today. Are they the only types? Not even close. But beginners would do well to wrap their heads around the first three we're about to look at.

First, though, why should we use different types of needles? Aren't they just long sticks? Yeah, they are long sticks but they are long sticks which have a distinct shape to them which makes it easier or harder to work with certain designs. We pick the needle we use based on the project we're about to undertake.

Straight Needles: Straight needles are the most common knitting needles. If you are looking to start knitting but don't want to invest in more than what is absolutely necessary then you should start with a pair of these. They have a pointed end which is used for creating the stitches and a stopper at the other end so that your yarn doesn't slide off.

These needles are most often found around the 10 to 12 inch range but they can be purchased in longer or shorter versions if you need to. They are made out of wood, steel, plastic or bamboo most often and these materials have their own positive and negative features, though many of these need to be discovered by the individual rather than being some sort of universal feature.

Straight needles are great for working on projects which are made flat such as washcloths. For projects that aren't going to be flat they can be used to create the flat sections which then get knit together to create the whole later on.

Circular Needles: Circular needles are best used for round projects, as you probably guessed from the name. Instead of being a rigid stick, these needles are attached with a cord that can easily flex and be twisted into a circular shape. Both needles are connected together by this cord.

KNITTING FOR BEGINNERS

These needles come in a larger size, typically ranging from 16 inches to as long as 48 inches. They can also be purchased in different sizes, though their use begins to dramatically change as you play around with size. The needles themselves tend to be of the same material as your straight needles but the cord that connects them will be made out of a nylon or a coated steel so that it holds onto the shape you twist it into.

You use these needles for projects that are round, like sweaters or hats. They can be used for flat projects but you're better off sticking with straight needles when this is the case.

Double-Point Needles: Double-point needles, often shortened to DPNs, are very short needles. They tend to average about six or seven inches in size and they are typically sold in sets containing four or six of them. They get their name from the fact that they are pointed into needles on both ends rather than just one side.

These needles are used for smaller projects such as knitting socks. They are also commonly used in knitting toys or smaller projects which require a high level of control. However, they are among the harder needles to use and so I recommend that beginners don't worry about them until they're proficiently using straight and circular needles.

Interchangeable Needles: Interchangeable needles are a fantastic option for when you want a flexible needle with many different ways of using them. These needles are connected with a cord but the pieces aren't stuck to the cord like they are with circular needles. Instead these needles can be swapped out and replaced with different makes so that you can change the style, size or length of your needles as you see fit.

In a lot of ways, this makes these less of a type of needle in and of themselves. They are more like a combination of the different needles we've looked at before. They offer the benefit of being able to switch out your needles but you still need to know which needle is right for the job to make the best use of them. Once a beginner has an understanding of when to reach for a larger or smaller needle, they'll be ready to purchase and benefit from an interchangeable needle.

Cable Needles: Cable needles are weird looking needles. They are pointed on both ends like a double-point needle is but the middle of the needle has an indentation which traps the yarn. These are used for knitting cables. You don't necessarily need to use a cable needle for knitting cables but they definitely make it the best experience.

These needles are easy to differentiate from the others we've looked at and I recommend that beginners ignore them until they are ready to start branching out into the world of cables.

Yarn

It's pretty hard to knit without some yarn. Not impossible, however, as there are types of knitting which use recycled t-shirts, leather or even glass. But 99% of the knitting you'll encounter out in the world, and 100% of the knitting we're looking at in this book, use yarn.

Yarn is the term we use to refer to any type of thread which has been spun for the purpose of textile work, such as knitting, sewing, weaving or crocheting. Many beginners think that yarn is some special type of fabric but the truth is that yarn can be made out of pretty much any fiber. You could use cotton from plants or the wool from a sheep. The fiber is spun to create a thread and it is then bundled together into balls, which is the state you will most often find it in when purchasing for yourself.

Yarn can come in many different styles. The common defining features of yarn are color, fiber type and weight. Color is a purely aesthetic choice and it doesn't have an effect on the act of knitting, only on the way the project ends up looking. Switching fibers will have a major difference on whatever you are knitting. Some fibers are more flexible than others, some are more heat resistant than others; there are all sorts of differences that arise from changing the fiber you are working with but more often this difference is most noticeable on the end project rather than in the act of knitting itself.

As far as directly affecting the knitting process, the weight of the yarn is going to be a crucial factor. Yarn which is heavy is going to need to be worked differently than a yarn of a lighter weight. This will also directly affect the way that the needles you are using feel. You may find that you need to change the size of your needles to better use a heavier or a lighter yarn. This is where discussions of gauge come into play.

Most patterns will tell you what type of yarn they are designed for. These tend to use a numeric system with each weight assigned a different number. These range from 0 to 7, or lightest to heaviest. These cover: Lace (0); Super fine (1); Fine (2); Light (3); Medium (4); Bulky (5); Super Bulky (6); and Jumbo (7).

Scissors

Scissors are one of those tools that you probably already have, but if you don't, then you're definitely going to need some. Getting a pair of scissors that can easily cut through jumbo yarn will make your life easier, since you won't need to worry about upgrading them down the road.

Scissors are used at the end of the project. When you finish your item, the yarn will still be attached to the ball from which it came. This is when we reach for our scissors and give the yarn a quick snip, leaving enough of a "tail" for us to work into the project. You will also find yourself reaching for the scissors when you want to switch colors during the project.

There isn't really much more that can be said about scissors. They just cut the yarn. But because they cut the yarn it is important that you aim to work with scissors that don't jam up or get caught when trying to cut fabric, otherwise they could damage the project. While chances are that they won't, there is a 100% chance that you'll get frustrated if they do. So purchase some quality scissors and save yourself a headache.

Tape Measure

A tape measure is always a useful tool. If you already have one then you'll be fine. It doesn't matter if it is a tape measure for construction use or one that is designed for fabric use. As long as you can measure things, you'll be alright. With that said, it is worth noting that a tape measure that can be bent easily is always a plus, as it'll make measuring round objects a much easier task.

There are two key reasons why a measuring tape is important. Pretend that you are looking to make a sweater but you aren't sure what size it needs to be. The pattern you have specifies a size, but you're not sure if it will fit your intended recipient. You can use a tape measure to measure their dimensions and then you can alter the pattern as needed for it to fit. If the pattern is laid out in stitches then all you need to do is take the tape measure and find out the dimensions of each row of stitches. You can then use these to determine how many rows you need to remove or add to the project so that it fits.

The other reason that a tape measure is a must is because there are plenty of patterns which don't tell you how many rows to use. Instead they tell you the size of the project in inches or centimeters. If you want to work on a pattern like this, then you need to be able to measure everything out properly or you're going to find yourself having a frustrating time guessing whether or not you're doing it right.

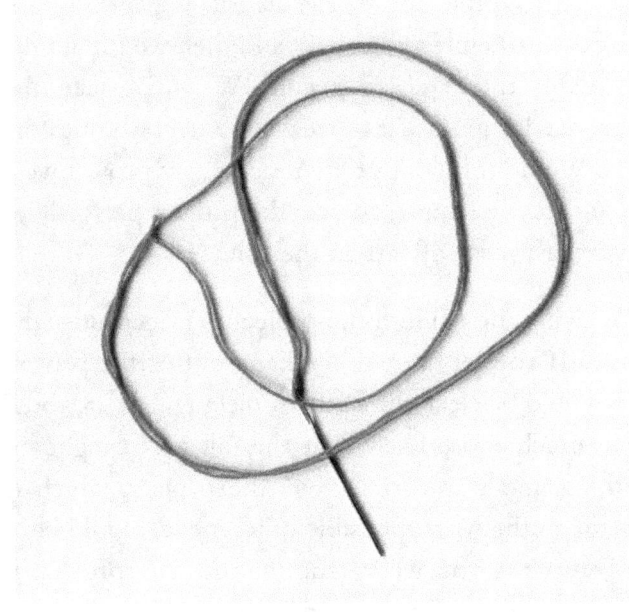

Tapestry Needle

A tapestry needle looks just like a sewing needle, only it is quite large. The eye of the needle needs to be large enough to fit even the bulkiest of yarn. But unlike your knitting needles, you only need a single tapestry needle. You may decide to purchase a couple different sizes of tapestry needles, especially when working with lace or super fine yarn but you only really need a single tapestry needle per size category.

Remember how we mentioned leaving a "tail" behind when using our scissors to cut the yarn? This tail is what we need the tapestry needle for. We cut the yarn with a tail of roughly a foot long and then we thread the tail through the tapestry needle. We then take the tapestry needle and use it to weave the tail back into the project. We do this with pretty much every project we'll make, unless we happen to size the project perfectly to use every last piece of yarn in the ball.

Weaving the tail into the project in effect hides the "seams." If you let the tail just hang out of the project then it would be clear where the project ended. It would also be much more likely that the tail gets caught on something and starts to unravel the project, which is pretty much the worst possible outcome we could have here. But when you weave the tail into the project, it hides where the project ends and it prevents that ending piece from getting caught and pulling everything apart.

This makes a tapestry needle one of the key pieces of equipment you should purchase when first getting into knitting.

Stitch Markers

Stitch markers look almost exactly like a safety pin, only they tend to have a much brighter color so that they stand out easily. They're rounded so that they can easily slip over your needles as need be. Some stitch markers are designed to be slotted directly into or onto a stitch.

As the name implies, their purpose is to mark your stitches.

Stitch markers can be extremely important depending on what you are making. Simple designs won't see much of a use for these, though that doesn't mean they aren't helpful. If you start a row with one type of stitch before moving into another then you may find it beneficial to use a stitch marker on that stitch so you know exactly where it is when you start knitting the next row. When used in this manner, even on the easiest of projects, they can really help you avoid one of the biggest mistakes beginners make: shrinking or growing rows. But we'll talk more about this type of mistake in chapter six.

For the time being I would recommend that you purchase some stitch markers. You should be able to get a dozen of them for a couple dollars, so they're only a drop in the bucket. Don't be afraid to use them, even on simple projects, if you feel like they could help. They're the type of gear that is used in a very personal manner. Your knitting needles are always used to make stitches but your stitch makers could be used to represent a dozen different things, it all depends on how you choose to place them and what stitches you consider important enough to mark for an easier time remembering them.

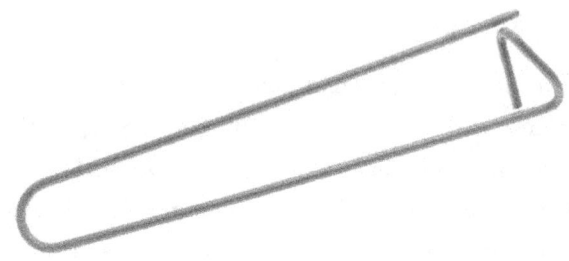

Stitch Holders

A stitch holder is like an even larger version of a stitch marker. They pretty much look the same since both of these pieces of equipment are designed based on safety pins. The goal of a stitch holder is to hold a stitch in place rather than just mark it.

With some projects you work on, you'll reach a point at which you need to leave some stitches out for later. For example, some sweater designs will have you work on the arm and then move outwards afterwards. From the arm the stitches move out in two directions but we can only work on one direction at a time. In this case, what we do is we use a stitch holder to hold onto the stitches we're not using so that we can come back to them later.

Stitch holders are super useful tools but they're not as commonly used as stitch markers. Nor are they overly common in patterns designed for beginners. They are quite cheap, however, and you may be interested in picking up a handful of them while doing your initial knitting gear purchase. But if you can't, don't worry. You can always hold off purchasing them until you encounter a pattern that needs them. Just remember to fully read your patterns before you start working on them. That way, you don't get to the point where you need a stitch holder before you've had a chance to purchase one.

Row Counter

A row counter is a simple electronic device with a button on it that you can press every time you finish a row. A variation of this design that can be especially useful attaches directly onto your knitting needle so that you never forget that it is present.

This tool is incredibly useful for when you're working on projects that have a lot of rows. Beginner projects mostly only use a handful of rows, upwards of 15 or so. But once you start to reach out into larger projects, you'll find that the row count can reach up into the hundreds or even the thousands, depending on what you are working on. It can get difficult to keep these numbers in your mind and many knitters will find themselves asking "Am I on row thirty-six or thirty-seven?".

When you have a row counter, you simply press the button after you finish a row and it keeps track of which row you are on, thus saving you from having to go back and count the rows again yourself. If you are working on a project which changes colors at certain rows, then a row counter is especially recommended. However, beginners can get by without purchasing a row counter for some time.

Needle Gauge

You won't need a needle gauge right out of the gate, as you're likely to start with only one or two sets of knitting needles, but you'll find a needle gauge to be useful before long. If you have lots of knitting needles of different sizes, or if you like to take your knitting kit out with you on the road, then a needle gauge is a must.

A needle gauge is a small piece of material that looks a little bit like a ruler except it has a bunch of holes in the middle. In fact, it looks a lot like a ruler because the sides of it can be used as one, too. A needle gage is just a ruler with some extra bits added. Those extra bits are the important pieces, at least for our purposes. The holes down the middle of the needle gauge start small and then get bigger and bigger. The holes correspond to the different sizes of knitting needles, so you can quickly check and see how large the needle you've grabbed is. If your knitting needles are unmarked then a needle gauge will make your life much easier. It can also be used to check the gauge on any unmarked needles you are thinking about purchasing.

A needle gauge is most often made out of metal, plastic or wood, but you can purchase them made out of unique materials like bamboo or horn if you like. They are great for portable kits since they let you gauge your needles on the fly but the measurements along the side also make life easier, especially when you don't have the room to pull out a full measuring tape (such as when you're knitting in your car).

Yarn Bobbins

If you're working with a few different types of yarns, then you're probably going to want to invest in a couple yarn bobbins. These are plastic frames which you wrap your yarn around. These end up looking a lot like the balls of yarn you've previously bought only there is a hook to hold them secure so that you can hang them up and easily store them.

Many people don't bother with bobbins when working with balls of yarn since they are already fairly well sorted, but once you've had to cut your yarn a few times you'll notice that you have lots of scrap yarn left over and it has a tendency to get all tangled up. A yarn bobbin is a great way to separate this scrap yarn and keep it nice and neat in your storage.

Another use for yarn bobbins, and one that you may want to consider using in tandem with your balls of yarn, is to wrap your yarn around them so that it is easier to pull it free. Sometimes you will find that your yarn just doesn't want to come free from the ball and you really need to tug at it to get any slack from it. This isn't a particularly harmful process, just an annoying one. Using a yarn bobbin can make it much easier to pull the yarn and thus save you the hassle of having to wrestle it free from the ball.

Yarn Threader

All of your projects are going to end with a tapestry needle to hide the tail of the yarn, that's pretty much a given. But sometimes this step is easier said than done. If you are using cotton or another type of yarn which is quite easy to maneuver, then you shouldn't have any problems. But trickier yarns, especially those like mohair, can prove to be quite difficult to thread. This is also the case when it comes to working with especially large yarn or small yarn.

A yarn threader is a cheap option to make this experience easier. You can purchase a yarn threader for under $2, so, if you have any interest in working with difficult fibers, then I highly recommend it. They are incredibly easy to use, too. A yarn threader either has a little loop on the end or a hook. Stick this part of the yarn threader through the eye of your tapestry needle and then stick the yarn through the threader. The threader will always be bigger than the eye of the needle so that it is easier to use. Once you have looped your yarn through the threader, all you need to do is pull the threader back out of the eye of the needle. The yarn is attached to the threader, so it is also pulled through the eye of the needle and then you can simply tie it off as needed. Just remember to detach the yarn from the threader before doing so.

Yarn Guide

A yarn guide is another simple tool that can make your knitting experience a lot easier, though it is definitely not one that you need off the bat. This tool often looks like a ring that you slip over your finger. There is another ring at the top of the guide and a second at the bottom. You run your yarn through these smaller rings to help keep it separated so that they don't get all tangled up.

If you are working on patterns that use two different colors, then a yarn guide is a must have item. They make it incredibly easy for you to keep your colors separated so that you can easily switch between them as you need to. If you are using a single color, then you won't need a yarn guide; neither do you need one or if you are using two colors that trade off from one row to another. But if you are working in patterns, such as white snowflakes against a black background, then a yarn guide will help.

With that said, you may still want to use a yarn guide even on a project with a single color because it will help you keep the tension in your yarn just right.

Needle Caps

Needle caps look like tiny road cones for your needles. They slip onto the end of the needles like little hats, thus they can be said to cap off the needle. Beginners often get confused by needle caps and it is always a funny sight to catch a beginner trying to knit while the caps are still on the needle. They're not meant to be used when knitting but rather they are designed to be slipped onto your needle when you finish for the day.

If you are working on a long project, then the chances are pretty high that you'll find yourself needing to leave some stitches on your knitting needles between sessions. If you just set your needles down, you risk the chance that the stitches will slip off of them at some point before your next session or even while you are picking up the needles to begin again. To avoid this, all you need to do is pop a needle cap onto your needle securely and you'll be able to rest easily, knowing the stitches are safe. The stitches can't slip off of the needle because the cap blocks them from doing so.

While these aren't designed to be used when knitting, you can use them as such if you have no other options. For example, you could use a needle cap to convert a double-point needle into a straight needle if you don't have any other way to get one. For the most part, you are better off using them as they are intended and simply getting your hands on another straight needle instead.

Chapter Summary

- There are quite a few tools which you should purchase if you are getting into knitting. But you could get away with just some circular needles, a tapestry needle and some yarn if you really had to.

- None of these tools are overly expensive or hard to find, so it should be no problem purchasing them.

- Knitting needles are used to hold the yarn and the stitches but there's actually several kinds.

- Straight needles are the kind you see the most often and they can be thought of as an all-around knitting needle.

- A circular needle is best used for projects which are circular, such as pullovers.

- Double-point needles are often incredibly small, making them great for small projects. As the name suggests, they have a point on both ends of the needle.

- Interchangeable needles are needles which can have the ends changed out to give the user a high level of versatility.

- Cable needles are two small needle ends that are connected with a cable between them that offers a lot of interesting possibilities for the projects you work on.

- Yarn is any type of thread which has been spun for the purpose of textile creation.

- Yarn comes in the following sizes: Lace (0); Super fine (1); Fine (2); Light (3); Medium (4); Bulky (5); Super bulky (6); and Jumbo (7).

- Scissors are used in pretty much every project since you need to cut the working yarn to separate your project from the ball of yarn.

- A tape measure isn't always important, but there are many patterns which call for a certain length or size rather than a specific number of rows or stitches.

- A tapestry needle is like a large sewing needle which we use to weave the yarn tail (that part left over after we use our scissors to cut the working yarn) into the project and secure it.

- Stitch markers are basically little safety pins which we use to mark specific stitches. Sometimes we need to come back to a stitch later or sometimes we need to leave ourselves a little reminder of what we're doing and that's where these come into play.

- Stitch holders are like larger versions of stitch markers which can be used to hold multiple stitches for later.

- A row counter is a simple electronic device which you click each time you finish a row so that it keeps track of which row you are on. There are row counter models which attach to your knitting needle, so you don't forget to use them.

- A needle gauge is a type of ruler that can be used for measurements but it also has holes throughout it so you can easily gauge the size of your needles, as the name implies.

- Yarn bobbins are little plastic frames which you wrap your yarn around to make it both easier to maintain the proper tension as well as keep everything neat and tidy.

- A yarn threader is an inexpensive tool which helps you easily thread your yarn into your tapestry needle.

- A yarn guide is a type of ring you slip over your finger to be able to keep the yarn in place while you're working it.

- Needle caps are little plastic cones which slip onto the ends of your knitting needles to hold the stitches in place whenever you need to pause an unfinished project.

KNITTING FOR BEGINNERS

In the next chapter, you will learn all about knit stitches and purl stitches. With these two stitch styles we are able to combine them to create all sorts of intricate stitch patterns that range from simple (but beautiful) to incredibly complex (and, obviously, also beautiful).

CHAPTER THREE

KNITTING PATTERNS

Between this chapter and the next you will learn what you need to start knitting your own projects. We're going to begin by first creating a slip knot so that we can cast on, which is the term we use to refer to the first loop on our knitting needles that then acts as the foundation of the project. Before we can worry about anything, we need to worry about this fundamental part.

After that, we will turn our attention over to the essential stitches which make up knitting. We'll start with basic stitches like the knit stitch and the purl stitch and we'll move into more complicated stitches like the moss stitch, double moss stitch, the 1/1 rib stitch and even the broken rib stitch (which isn't as nasty or painful as it sounds). Knitting is all about learning how to bring these stitches together, how to combine them in such a way as to make interesting patterns and create wonderful works of textile art.

KNITTING FOR BEGINNERS

Practice each of these stitches in turn. Start at the beginning and work your way through them, making sure that you master one before moving onto the next. This will slow down your experience with the book but it will greatly improve your knitting abilities and make it that much easier to follow along and make the projects we'll be exploring in chapter five.

Slip Knot and Casting On

Before we can start to knit, we need to cast on. There are several ways of doing this but we're going to be starting with a slip knot and then using the "knit cast-on" technique. This is a great way for beginners to practice casting off because you can actually use it to practice your knit stitches, as we'll be showing in a moment.

First we need a slip knot. A slip knot is one of the most useful things you can learn how to make. We'll use it at the start of each of our projects when knitting, but it can also be useful when crocheting or even when you're out camping. It's just an extremely versatile technique and one that you'll master quickly.

Start by taking the tail of the yarn in your hand so that it is dangling against your palm. Next, use your other hand to take the yarn and wrap it clockwise behind your index and pointer fingers. Grab the part of yarn that is still attached to the ball of yarn and slide it under and through the loop you've made around your fingers. Carefully slide this loop off of your fingers and give it a gentle pull to tighten it up as you slide it onto your needle.

Every time you need to attach thread to your needle, this is the technique that you'll be reaching for. From here we move into casting on with our knit stitch.

To cast on with a knit stitch, we need the needle with the slip knot on it in our left hand. This means that our right hand will have the needle that is empty. This is the approach for right-handed knitters and if you're left-handed, simply reverse this for the same purpose. We start to cast on by first sticking the empty needle into the loop of the needle in your left hand. Start at the front and work towards the back. We call this opening the loop and we're going to spend more time with this technique in just a moment.

Once the right-hand needle has been worked through the loop you will then take the yarn from the ball, also known as the working yarn, and drape this over the point of the right-hand needle in a counter-clockwise fashion. It is important that you only loop the working yarn over the right-hand needle and not both, otherwise this technique won't work. This approach to knitting, with the yarn in your right hand, is called English knitting. We sometimes refer to this as "throwing." If we were to work with the yarn in our left hand instead, then it would be called continental knitting. However, keep in mind that these styles are reversed for left-handed people. A left-handed knitter holding the yarn in their left hand would still be English knitting.

The next step is to move the right-hand needle down so that gravity pulls the loop down. You want the loop on the needle to get down close to the tip, but you don't want to lose it. At the same time, you need to move the right-hand needle out from its location behind the left-hand needle. The second the right-hand needle is out from behind the left-hand needle, push it forward again so that it is in front of the left needle. This technique might sound complicated when it is broken down into individual movements but what you are doing here is allowing the loop you made to get close to the tip of the needle while also bringing that needle from its position behind the left-hand needle to be in front of it. It's almost like the gears of a machine at work and it is a very simple movement that you will be making all the time, so it is important to practice it often. You may find it tricky at first, but you'll master it before long.

What this movement has done is create a new stitch, a knit stitch actually, but you need to finish it by adding it to the needle. If you don't then you'll lose it. This loop was made on the right-hand needle so you'll want to add it to the left-hand needle, just after the slip knot. We do this by slipping the loop around the left-hand needle and pulling the right-hand needle out from it. This part of the step is a little different from the normal knit stitch. We are casting the stitches here onto the left needle and they will serve as the foundation for the piece to come next; we'll be knitting stitches together using these stitches that have been cast on to the left-hand needle. For now, just slip that loop onto the left-hand needle but be careful to make sure that you add the loop to the needle in the same direction each time. Once you start changing directions, the project will begin to get more complicated. Harder projects may have you alter the direction of casting on, but for beginners we want to keep it as consistent as possible.

This step can be repeated over and over again as needed. How many stitches you need on the left-hand needle will be greatly determined by the pattern and project that you are working on. Once you have finished casting on all of the stitches you need, it will be time to start your project and begin worrying about stitches instead of cast-on stitches.

Knit Stitch

We technically just learned the knit stitch, but we did some while casting on, which is a little bit different than using the stitch itself. As this stitch is pretty much the first and most important stitch that beginners learn on their knitting journey, it is worth taking a moment to reflect on it a bit longer and to see how it looks aside from casting on. You'll find yourself using this stitch in pretty much every beginner's pattern you find, so it is worth the practice.

Begin by first getting your slip knot onto your needle and then casting on a dozen or so stitches. We need to cast on our stitches, as we use these cast on stitches to form the stitches of the next row. Since we used the knitted cast on, you've already got some training with this one so you should have no problem rocking the following steps.

We start by opening the loop of the stitch closest to the end of the left-hand needle, which is the needle that has all of the stitches which we previously cast on. We slip the end of the right-hand needle into the first loop, making sure to go from the front and out the back. The loops on your left-hand needle should be facing you and the bumpy part of those loops should be pointed at your body.

Once the right-hand needle is through the first loop, take your yarn and wrap it over the needle. Remember that we are only going over the right needle and that we're doing it by wrapping counter-clockwise around it. If you've done it properly, then you'll have a tiny loop on your right-hand needle and the working yarn will have nestled into the space where the right and left needles meet. We then work that movement we practiced to slip the right-hand needle from behind the left-hand needle so that it ends up in front of it. Remember that, as you make this movement, you want the right-hand needle to point down a bit so that the loop gets as close to the end of the needle as possible.

Now we finish the stitch off by moving the right-hand needle up enough that the loop on the left-hand needle slips off. This finishes the knit stitch and you can then move onto the next stitch on the left-hand needle. We continue this until we get to the end of loops on the left-hand needle. At this point, you'll notice that the right-hand needle is now filled with loops. We take the work and flip it over. If we had been working on the front, we're now working on the back. At the same time, switch hands so that you are now holding the right-hand needle in your left hand and vice versa. You have now switched onto the next row and you can continue knitting it together exactly as before.

Working this stitch becomes an almost robotic pattern. You slip the right-hand needle into the front loop of the left needle and you wrap your working yarn over the right-hand needle in a counter-clockwise fashion. The right-hand needle is then pulled back under the left-hand needle and pushed over top of it and then pulled to the right to slip the stitch off the left-hand needle. This is repeated again and again until you reach the end of the row. It's almost exactly the same as creating the cast on, except that we finish each stitch by transferring it from the left needle over to the right needle.

Purl Stitch

Next up is the purl stitch. This stitch and the knit stitch together make up two sides of the same coin. They're similar in their opposite natures. If you make row after row of knit stitches then you'll find that they take on an alternating pattern in which the first, third and fifth rows look slightly different from the second and fourth rows. This is because of the way we flip over the project to get to the next row. The front and the back of these stitches look different from each other, so, even though we used one stitch we have the appearance of two stitches.

The purl stitch actually looks like the back of the knit stitch; you can give your project a more uniform appearance by switching from the knit stitch to the purl stitch between rows. When it comes time to move onto the next row, switch back over to the knit stitch and you'll end up with a project that looks like a single, uniform stitch but it is actually composed of two different types of stitches. By making this the second type of stitch you learn, you can benefit from this bit of knitting trickery so that even your beginning projects look absolutely professional.

Assuming that you have already cast on, the first step with the purl stitch is to push the right-hand needle into the loop of the stitch that is closest to the end of the left-hand needle. Normally, we enter from the front of the stitch and push to the back, keeping our working yarn in the back so that we can easily wrap it over the needle. This time around, we're going to enter into the stitch beginning from the right and moving to the left so that it enters from the back and exits from the front. The working yarn is kept in the front, too, so that it is easier to work it over the needle. Previously, at this step, you would have the right needle under the left, but this time around you end up with the right needle in front, over the left needle.

With your right-hand needle pushed through the loop in this manner, take your working yarn and pull it over your right-hand needle. You're still going to come up and over the needle in a counter-clockwise manner, but remember that the working yarn is in front this time. With the yarn looped over the right-hand needle in this manner, it should still slip into that space where the left and right needle meet each other. As with the previous stitch, it is this position of the working yarn that we want with every stitch; otherwise we've messed something up and the stitches aren't going to function properly.

With the yarn worked over the right-hand needle in a counter-clockwise manner, it is time to jump into that robotic movement that we'll be making regularly. This movement is what moves our stitch from the left needle onto the right needle; we need to master it if we want to rock this row. Just slide your right-hand needle backwards, so that the loop starts to move towards the tip, careful so that we don't slide it off entirely. Previously we moved the right-hand needle from the back of the left-hand needle to the front; this time we're doing the opposite and so our right-hand needle comes back and away from the left-hand needle just enough that we can slip it underneath the left-hand needle to the back. If done properly, then the right-hand needle should be behind the left-hand needle, but the original loop should be on the left-hand needle while there is a new loop on the right-hand one. Again, the working yarn is in front of the needles and not behind them. All that is left now is to use the right-hand needle to slip the loop off the left-hand needle; we do this by pulling the right-hand needle up and away from the left-hand needle, towards the tip of the needle. You'll have a new loop on the right-hand needle but one less loop on the left-hand needle.

This gives you a single purl stitch. Continue by repeating the steps with the next loop on the left-hand needle and continuing in this manner until you either make it to the end of the row or until you need to switch to a different stitch as the pattern calls for.

Stockinette Stitch

The stockinette stitch isn't actually a stitch in and of itself. It is actually more of a pattern that is made from putting different stitches together. In this case, the two stitches are the knit stitch and the purl stitch. Bringing the two together in alternating rows is called the stockinette stitch. Since we've learned both the knit stitch and the purl stitch, we should have no issue with quickly mastering the stockinette stitch.

It doesn't matter how many stitches your project uses, you could have a single stitch and still make the stockinette stitch. What matters is that the project in question uses multiple rows. If you have a pattern that uses an even or odd number of stitches, it makes no difference. In fact, you could have either an even or an odd number of rows and it wouldn't matter. We associate a row of several stitches with the stockinette stitch because most projects use rows with more than just a handful of stitches.

To rock the stockinette stitch, begin your project with a row of knit stitches. This is often referred to as knitting or knitting across. When you finish that row, you move into the purl stitch. This is often referred to as purling across. At the end of your purl row you start the new row with knit stitches and then continue this alternating pattern. The look that this pattern gives you is often called "knit fabric." It's an extremely common pattern, so much so that you'll find it used in just about every type of knitting pattern you can find. Hats, sweaters, towels, pretty much anything can be made using the stockinette stitch for an incredibly easy but beautiful looking design.

A variation of the stockinette stitch is the reverse stockinette stitch. This stitch pattern is made by starting with a row of purl stitches and then alternating to the knit stitches. Therefore a stockinette stitch begins with the knit stitches before the purl stitches and the reverse stockinette stitch just reverses this (as the name would imply).

Be prepared to use this stitch pattern a lot. In fact, you could pretty much stop learning new types of stitches here and still manage to make some high-quality and beautiful looking textile creations. But why stop when things are going so well? Besides, we also learned what is needed for the garter stitch, so next we'll give it a look.

Garter Stitch

Here we have the truly easiest of the stitch patterns which you'll be using. It is called the garter stitch and it is entirely made out of knit stitches. That's right, all you need for this design is to know a single stitch and we've already covered that in detail, so we won't be going over it again.

In short, the garter stitch is what we call it when we use knitting stitches in every row. We add a knit stitch to every stitch in our row until we get to the end. At the end of the row we flip the project over and then start the next row using knitting stitches in every loop again. If we continue in this pattern until the end of the project then we've used garter stitch throughout the project.

If you have gotten to the purl stitch but still don't feel comfortable enough with it to make a stockinette stitch then you should practice your garter stitch more. You can make towels, scarves and other simple projects with this stitch alone. While the garter stitch doesn't look bad, per se, it certainly doesn't have the charm of a stockinette stitch. The stockinette stitch isn't particularly difficult, so many beginners should be able to skip over the garter stitch to speed up their learning curve.

Rib Stitching

Ribbing is a lot more complicated than the garter stitch and a little bit more complex when compared to the stockinette stitch. This is a form of alternating stitch pattern that uses the knitting stitch and the purl stitch but rather than alternating between rows it alternates within the row. It is named for the way that end product seems to be ribbed. That is to say, it creates a pattern in which a line of stitches comes out from the fabric, then it sinks in, then another line is pushed out. Since the pattern continues across multiple rows, it creates a vertical effect, whereas the garter stitch and the stockinette stitch create a horizontal one.

We refer to any pattern in which alternating knit stitches and purl stitches lineup to create the appearance of columns as rib stitching. However, there are all sorts of different variations of the rib stitch, as you'll see listed below. Rib stitches are named after the way that the stitches alternate. This means that the 1/1 rib stitch alternates on a one to one level, but the 2/2 rib stitch uses a two to two level. It is important to pay attention to how many stitches will be in a row when you are picking an appropriate rib stitch to use. If you select a large rib stitch but don't have enough space to finish the pattern properly then the whole effect is going to be ruined.

1/1 Rib Stitch

This is the most basic of the rib stitches you can work with as it alternates between one knit stitch and one purl stitch back and forth. Using this approach will give you columns that are quite thin but there will be many of them traveling up and down the project. It's a good stitch for those that are looking to create an effect of stitches held quite closely together.

While you will likely want to jump straight in and start alternating your stitches immediately, this isn't always the best case. It is often a better idea to work the sides in a simple pattern that repeats on every row. This helps you ensure that the rows have enough stitches for your chosen rib, but also it helps to keep them looking neat and proper.

For a basic 1/1 rib stitch you'll want a simple edging effect. We're actually going to select an odd number of stitches for our rows so we can edge them properly. Start your row with a knit stitch. By doing this with each row, our edge is going to be sharp and defined and we can be sure that our project isn't shrinking or growing between rows (a common mistake that beginners make). So the row begins with a knit stitch but we're not going to start alternating yet. In the second stitch from the side, work in another knit stitch. Now we will start to alternate; so, next is a purl stitch, then a knit stitch, then a purl stitch and so on until we get close to the end. Once we get near the end of the row we want to pay attention to the last two stitches of the row. Our row started with two knit stitches and so we want to end it with two knit stitches. If we have selected a properly sized row then the last three stitches on the row should be a purl stitch, a knit stitch and a second knit stitch.

That gives us our first row of stitches and it is at this point we need to be the most careful. We could easily mess up our first row, because it is at this point that we are setting the pattern for the next one. The second row and all of them that follow thereafter are thus simple to do because you just need to put in the same type of stitch in the right place. This means that the pattern you follow will look exactly the same as the first row, which will act like a visual guide. Continue adding rows this way until you reach the end.

2/2 Rib Stitch

A 2/2 rib stitch is a more complicated pattern. For this one, we want our rows to be a multiple of four plus four. This means that we can't do it twice with a row of eight. We could divide eight by four to get two but then we wouldn't have the room for the extras. We could work four into eight one time and have enough left over to close out our sides but then this wouldn't be a very interesting looking piece. Our best bet is to use a 2/2 rib stitch for a project that uses large rows.

The first row of a 2/2 rib stitch begins with a single knit stitch. Again, this will serve as the edge of the project before we start alternating. This time around we are going to alternate on a larger scale and so work a knit stitch into the second and the third place. You should have three knit stitches in a row coming from this side, which is important to note for later. But for now we move into that alternating flow by using a purl stitch for the next two, so that now we have five stitches made, three knit stitches and two purl stitches. Continue in the pattern adding two knit stitches and then two purl stitches until you come to the last three slots of the row. If it is sized properly then you should finish two purl stitches and see that you have three slots left. Fill the first two slots with knit stitches. This should give the appearance that you're going to be continuing the pattern but what it is actually doing is serving as a reflection of the start of the row. With the one remaining slot left, add in another knit stitch, bringing the total up to three knit stitches at the end of the row. This last stitch is the edge stitch; the two stitches before last give the piece the reflective feature that makes it a higher-quality creation.

Then, as you go forward, it is just like with the 1/1 rib stitch where everything is now laid out for you and you simply need to recreate the stitches as you add rows. When you come to a purl stitch, you add another purl stitch. When you're working into a knit stitch, you add another knit stitch. Just keep this up and add rows in this manner until you reach the end of the project.

2/2 Garter Stitch Rib

The 2/2 garter stitch rib is a variation of the 2/2 rib stitch. You can use it in place of the 2/2 rib stitch, so check that entry for notes on how many stitches you need in each row. This is a really beautiful looking stitch, vastly more interesting than the typically 2/2 rib stitch. It achieves its beauty through the way that it combines alternating rows with alternating stitches in order to create a pattern that is both horizontal and vertical at the same time.

The secret to this stitch is that it works out alternating rows. We begin with a row that consists entirely of knit stitches. Since these are the easiest stitches to do, you should have no problem with this first row. Just remember that the size of the row is important. The second row is going to begin with a knit stitch to serve as the edge like normal. But this time around we're going to switch things up by then making two purl stitches. The start to this row will be a knit stitch, a purl stitch and a second purl stitch. From here, we're going to move into a repeating pattern of two knit stitches followed by two purl stitches. This pattern is repeated all throughout this row until we come to the last stitch in the row. This brings us back to our edge and, so, we're going to add a knit stitch. This time around we don't need to worry about including half of a round like we did with the 2/2 rib stitch because we're ending on two purl stitches and a knit stitch instead of three knit stitches.

Here is where things change. With either the 1/1 rib stitch or the 2/2 rib stitch, we would then continue this pattern of stitching when we want to work on another row. But not so here. We started with a row that was entirely knit stitches. Our second row then had the 2/2 rib stitch pattern to it. For our third row, we're going back to the basics and we're using knit stitches in every space. So now we have three rows, two of them are the same but the middle row is different. As we start on the fourth row, we will recreate the same pattern we used in the second row. This means our fourth row will be a knit stitch, two purl stitches, then two knit stitches followed by two purl stitches repeating until we get to the last spot and use a knit stitch to complete the edge.

By alternating this pattern in such a way we get a really cool looking pattern. The raised columns of the ribbed design will still stand out boldly and proudly but now the sunken section between them will have stitches that almost look like chains holding the whole thing together. In this way, the 2/2 garter stitch rib is one of the coolest stitch patterns that you can learn to make and doing so will take you well past being a beginner.

Broken Rib Stitch

The broken rib stitch is basically the 2/2 garter stitch rib but achieved with a 1/1 rib style. For this technique to work you want your rows to be the right size for a 1/1 rib stitch. Please check out those calculations in the 1/1 rib stitch section above.

We're going to start the broken rib stitch much like the last one; we're going to make our first row entirely out of knit stitches. Once we get to the second row, we'll begin the rib stitch much as expected, by first using a knit stitch to serve as our edge. For our second stitch, we'll use a purl stitch. From here, we move into the repeating pattern of one knit stitch followed by one purl stitch and we follow this through all the way to the last stitch. You've already guessed that the last stitch is a knit stitch to serve as our edge. With this pattern, you could basically think of it as repeating right out of the gate. After all, you start with a single knit stitch and a single purl stitch before entering into a repeating pattern. But we don't refer to these first two as part of the repeating section, because it is important that we realize the purpose of the knit stitch is to give us our edge.

At this point we have two rows. The first row is entirely knit stitches and the second row is a version of the 1/1 rib stitch. You might have already guessed that the third row is going to be entirely made up of knit stitches again. If so, congrats for getting it right! When you get to the end of the third row and begin the fourth, simply repeat the pattern from the second row. When adding rows to a broken rib stitch, think of the rows in pairs of two. You want to add a row that is all knits and a row that is ribs, always in a pair. You might decide to close out the project with a different stitch design on the top or by ending it after an entirely knit stitch row, but other than this, the broken rib stitch pattern works in alternating rows with two rows completing a single pass.

Seed Stitch

The seed stitch is another form of the rib stitch but with a major difference thrown into the mix. If you are going to work with the seed stitch then you can work it with a 1/1 rib stitch or a 2/2 rib stitch; it won't be a very good fit for the broken rib or the garter rib stitch. It could still be used in these, but the effect it would create wouldn't be nearly as attractive as the seed stitch, the garter rib stitch or the broken rib stitch are on their own. Use the guides for the 1/1 or 2/2 rib stitch to decide on how many stitches should be in each row. We'll use the 1/1 rib stitch for this example.

For your first row, make a 1/1 rib stitch pattern. This is a knit stitch for the edge. Next add a knit stitch and then a purl stitch and repeat this pattern until you come to the last two stitches in the row. Add a knit stitch twice to create the mirroring effect and to work as the edge.

Normally we would continue the next row in this same pattern to complete our rib stitching, but this time we're looking to do a seed stitch. We're still going to start the second row with a knit stitch to serve as our edge. But instead of following this first knit stitch with a second knit stitch, we're going to follow it with a purl stitch. In our third slot we're going to work in another knit stitch, then another purl stitch, another knit stitch, another purl stitch and so on until the end, where we'll use a knit stitch for the edge.

To continue this pattern we simply return to the positions in our first row when we're working the third, then we repeat the second row when we work on the fourth row. What happens here is that we use a knit stitch into every purl stitch and a purl stitch into every knit stitch, except for our edges, which continue to be knit stitches.

This pattern doesn't necessarily need to have an edge. None of them do, really, but they help to make the project look better. If you aren't using an edge, you could work this pattern with an even or an odd number of stitches in each row with just some minor tweaks. A seed stitch with an even number of stitches per row starts with a knit stitch, then a purl stitch; it repeats this pattern until the end of the row. When starting the next row, you would begin with a purl stitch and then alternate between knit stitches until the end. If you are working with an odd number of stitches in each row then you begin with a knit stitch and alternate until the last stitch, which will be a knit stitch. The next row would then repeat the pattern and you would continue in this manner till done.

Moss Stitch

The moss stitch is quite similar to the seed stitch, so much, in fact, that you might be tricked into thinking it was the same stitch if you didn't pay close attention when being taught it. This stitch works on an alternating pattern with the placement of the knit stitches and the purl stitches changing places depending on what row they're in. The difference here is that the moss stitch works on a larger scale, as compared to the seed stitch. Both stitches are going to have a similar appearance, which makes them a good fit for many projects. For this stitch, you'll want to have enough slots in your row for a 1/1 pattern with three slots left over to create a symmetrical edge.

Start with your edge by making a single knit stitch. This is then followed by the repeating pattern of one knit stitch followed by one purl stitch. Repeat this until you get to the last two stitches in the row, at which point you will add a knit stitch for symmetry's sake and then finish with a knit stitch for the edging. On the second row you're going to do the same thing, as if you were making a ribbed pattern. So start with a knit stitch for the edge, alternate between a knit stitch and a purl stitch until you get to the last two spots in the row, at which point you will finish with a knit stitch for symmetry and then a knit stitch for the edging.

This is where this pattern gets different. On the third row, you are going to begin with a knit stitch. This is for the edging and so you're going to use knit stitches for the first and last stitch in the row no matter what. But instead of going into a second knit stitch, move into a purl stitch. Then add a knit stitch and continue this pattern until you get to the end of the row, at which point you should be able to just finish the pattern. If it is done properly then the first three stitches in the row will be a knit stitch, a purl stitch and a knit stitch and the last three stitches should be a knit stitch, a purl stitch and a knit stitch.

The fourth row is going to copy the third row, so this means that you'll add knit stitches to the spots that are knit stitched and purl stitches to the spots that have been purl stitched. But the fifth row changes things up again. This time we're going to go back to the pattern established in the first two rows, so knit stitch for the edge followed by a repeating pattern of one knit stitch then a purl stitch until you get to the end of the row and finish with two knit stitches. Repeat this pattern again for the sixth row. Going forward you will alternate your rows in this manner, first doing two rows that repeat knit stitch, purl stitch and then two rows which repeat purl stitch, knit stitch. Continue this four row pattern until the end of the project.

Little Granite Stitch

Here's a more complicated pattern. Those that we've looked at so far have worked on alternating rows or stitches with a very clear pattern. The little granite stitch alternates both rows and stitches, but it does so in a decidedly unbalanced way, making it much harder for beginners to master. The hard part of this one isn't so much the stitches, as we work with knit stitches and purl stitches throughout. Rather the hard part is keeping track of the number of stitches you've already done. This is because it uses a three to one repeating stitch pattern and, for some reason, this has the tendency to trip beginners up. Don't worry if you don't get it right away, a little practice will get you there.

For this particular stitch pattern you are going to use a repeating pattern of four stitches, so you'll want to be able to divide your row by four. Of course, we'll also want one stitch on each side for the purpose of edging but we'll actually want an extra three stitches to create symmetry. This means that we'll want to have a row that is a multiple of four with an extra five. So we'll want to have 9, 13, 17, 21 or 25 spots per row.

Begin the first row with your single knit stitch for the edge. From there, we'll move straight into the repeating pattern. Purl stitch the next three spots and then finish off with a single knit stitch. This is our four stitch pattern. We'll continue it by repeating three purl stitches, one knit stitch, three purl stitches, one knit stitch. This goes on until we get to the last four stitches in the row. Funnily enough, this actually will have the effect of continuing the pattern here because we want three purl stitches for symmetry and a knit stitch for the edge. So we can technically just repeat the pattern until the end of the row.

For the second row, simply repeat what you've done in the first row. Start with your knit stitch edge, then repeat the pattern of three purl stitches followed by a knit stitch until you get to the end of the row and finish with three purl stitches and the single knit stitch edge.

The third row is where we're going to stitch it up. As always, we're going to begin with a single knit stitch for our edging. But now we're going to get into a weird pattern. Rather than just invert the pattern like we did with the moss or seed stitches, we're going to instead make an entirely new pattern. This one will be one purl stitch followed by a single knit stitch followed by two purl stitches. So the pattern will be purl stitch, knit stitch, purl stitch, purl stitch. We continue this pattern right up until the last four stitches in the row. Here we want that symmetry and so we're going to go purl stitch, knit stitch, purl stitch. This leaves us with just the final spot and you've already guessed that it'll be a single knit stitch for the edging.

The fourth row will follow this pattern so it begins with a knit stitch then alternates purl stitch, knit stitch, two purl stitches until it gets to the end and finishes with a purl stitch, a knit stitch, a purl stitch and then a knit stitch for the edging.

The fifth row will then return to the pattern from the first row and so will the sixth row. The seventh row will copy the third row and the eighth row will copy the seventh. In this manner, this stitch functions across four rows and so you should continue, keeping the project's total number of rows as a multiple of four.

Basket Weave Stitch

Let's finish this chapter with the hardest stitch yet. This one is definitely beyond the level of a beginner, so if you can master this then you should consider yourself an intermediate knitter (as long as you've completed a handful of beginner projects). The reason that this one is so difficult is because the pattern requires twelve rows. That's right, this stitch pattern uses twelve rows and so a twenty-four row project would only have two instances of the stitch. This makes it three times as large as the next largest we've taken a look at, so don't worry if you find it a little intimidating right now. You can always come back and try it after you finish a few of the projects from chapter five.

KNITTING FOR BEGINNERS

For this pattern we're going to use a multiple of six, with four stitches for our symmetry and edging. This means that it works in rows of 10, 16, 22, 28, 34, and so on. Considering that it requires a large number of stitches per row and many rows, this stitch is best used for big projects like blankets, pillows or scarves. There are actually a few ways to do this pattern. Some recommend beginning with a knit stitch, four purl stitches, a knit stitch pattern and moving to a two purl stitches, two knit stitches, two purl stitches pattern at the end. We're going to use the second pattern, which turns into a three purl stitch, two knit stitch, one purl stitch repetition. The main thing here is that you're working multiples of six in your repetitions.

The first row of the basket weave stitch is incredibly easy. All you need to do is knit stitch along each of the pieces in the row. Technically, the first and the last stitch are there as edging. If you were doing it without edging, it would be exactly the same. The second row is almost just as easy. This time around you're going to use a single knit stitch as the first stitch in the row and a single knit stitch for the last stitch in the row but the rest of the row will be entirely purl stitches. So, now we have one row of knit stitches and one row of purl stitches. This is where it gets complicated.

The third row begins with a knit stitch for the edge. Next we'll work on a repeating pattern of two knit stitches followed by four purl stitches. This will end up being knit stitch, knit stitch, purl stitch, purl stitch, purl stitch, purl stitch. Repeat this pattern until you get to the last three stitches in the row. Here we want that symmetry so we knit stitch three times. This is two knit stitches to reflect the two earlier in the row and one knit stitch for the edging.

The fourth row works as the inverse of the third row. We start and finish with our single knit stitch edges, of course. But in the middle we're going to do the inverse by repeating a pattern of two purl stitches followed by four knit stitches. This gives us purl stitch, purl stitch, knit stitch, knit stitch, knit stitch, knit stitch. At the end, we'll close out with two purl stitches and our knit stitch edge.

The fifth row is a reflection of the third row and the sixth row is the reflection of the fourth row. This means that from row three to six we've created an alternating pattern.

Row seven is entirely knit stitches. Row eight is all purl stitches, except for our beginning and ending knit stitch edging.

With row nine we move back into a more complicated pattern again. This one uses the six part repeating pattern like rows three to six did, but this time the pattern is different. Begin with a knit stitch for your edging. From there start your repeating pattern, which this time around is three purl stitches, two knit stitches and then one purl stitch. This will give us purl stitch, purl stitch, purl stitch, knit stitch, knit stitch, purl stitch. When we get to the last three slots in the row, we work in two purl stitches for symmetry and a knit stitch for edging.

Row ten will then serve as the inverse of row nine. Start with your knit stitch edge. The repeating pattern we're using this time is then three knit stitches, two purl stitches followed by one last knit stitch. This gives us knit stitch, knit stitch, knit stitch, purl stitch, purl stitch, knit stitch. When we come to the last three slots in the row we work in three knit stitches, two for symmetry and one for the edge.

Row eleven repeats the pattern from row nine. Row twelve repeats the pattern from row ten. As you finish row twelve you'll have completed one basket weave stitch. It's a big one and a complicated one, so let's quickly go over it one more time.

The first row is entirely knit stitches. The second row is entirely purl stitches. Row three uses two knit stitches and then four purl stitches. Row four uses two purl stitches and then four knit stitches. Row five repeats row three. Row six repeats row four. Row seven is entirely knit stitches, repeating row one. Row eight is entirely purl stitches, repeating row two. Row nine is three purl stitches, two knit stitches and then a single purl stitch. Row ten is three knit stitches, two purl stitches and one knit stitch. Row eleven repeats row nine. Row twelve repeats row ten.

Don't worry if this stitch takes lots of practice to do right. It's not easy. But practice is always beneficial to you as a developing knitter.

KNITTING FOR BEGINNERS

Chapter Summary

- A slip knot is the first thing we need to learn if we want to knit. We use a slip knot to attach our yarn to our knitting needle in the first place.

- After our slip knot we then cast on, which is the term we use for making little stitches on our left-hand knitting needle. These cast on stitches give us a foundation from which to begin knitting our first row.

- The knit stitch is one of the two most common stitches used in knitting. It is an incredibly easy stitch in which we push the right-hand needle into a stitch from the front to the back, yarn over our needle and then pull it through.

- The front of a knit stitch is not quite flat but the back of a knit stitch is quite puffy. The back of a knit stitch is a purl stitch. To make a purl stitch we enter our stitches from the back to the front.

- By mixing knit stitches with purl stitches we are able to create tons and tons of intricate stitch patterns such as those that follow.

- The stockinette stitch is a pattern which starts with a row of knit stitches, followed by a row of purl stitches.

- The garter stitch is an incredibly easy stitch pattern as it entirely uses knit stitches. Just use a

KNITTING FOR BEGINNERS

knit stitch in every spot of every row to rock this pattern.

- Rib stitching is a technique in which we lineup stitches that use an alternating pattern so that they create a column-like effect.

- A 1/1 rib stitch is a simple rib stitching technique in which we alternate between knit stitches and purl stitches with a one knit, one purl pattern.

- A 2/2 rib stitch is a more complicated rib stitching technique which alternates between two knit stitches and two purl stitches.

- A 2/2 garter stitch rib is a rib stitch that works with alternating rows as well as a 2/2 rib stitch pattern.

- A broken rib stitch is a 2/2 garter stitch rib but done with a 1/1 rib stitch alternating repetition.

- A seed stitch is a rib stitch that can be worked with either 1/1 or 2/2 but each row knits into the opposite stitch so that knit stitches are used on purl stitches and purl stitches are used on knit stitches.

- The moss stitch is like a seed stitch but the moss stitch is achieved using a larger scale, often two rows of the same pattern before switching to two rows of the opposite pattern.

- The little granite stitch is a pattern which alternates both rows and stitches but in an unbalanced manner which can make it quite difficult for beginners to master.

- The basket weave stitch is an advanced stitch pattern which requires twelve rows in order to complete one pass of the pattern.

In the next chapter, you will learn about many of the essential techniques which fall outside of the purview of this chapter. These range from changing your yarn in the middle of a project to using a different color through to how to cast off at the end of a project. We'll look at how to weave the yarn tail into your creation and how to sew the seams when you need to. Along with this, we'll be fixing mistakes, such as dropped stitches or holes. We'll also examine a glossary of knitting terminology and abbreviations.

CHAPTER FOUR

ESSENTIAL TECHNIQUES

The title of this chapter is a little bit of a joke. These techniques are certainly essential but the truth is that you've just learned the most important parts of knitting in the last chapter! That's right, at this point you can consider yourself a fairly accomplished beginner. But there is more to learn and the use of the word essential is certainly not made entirely in jest.

In this chapter, we're going to cover elements and techniques of knitting that we haven't had a chance to go over yet. These include binding off and finishing our projects by weaving the ends or sewing the seams. This chapter will also cover how to fix mistakes as they crop up; which, unfortunately, will happen more often than we'd care to admit. But as long as we know how to fix them, we don't have to tell anyone else. Of course we'll cover other topics as well, so definitely stick around to check them out.

One important thing that has to be mentioned is that we're going to cover knitting terminology and abbreviations. Knitting is one of those skills that uses a ton of abbreviations and unique lingo, so it is important to go over this. It's a lot like crochet and the other forms of textile creation in this sense. We'll close out with a glossary covering these terms so that you can always return to this chapter whenever you find a term in a pattern that you don't know.

Binding Off (Also Known as Casting Off)

As you've worked the stitch patterns from the last chapter, we left out a key phase in any project: the end. Since we were just practicing our stitches, it wasn't important to bind off the pieces. But if we're going to move from practicing stitches to making projects, we're going to need to master this essential technique.

When you finish with the last row of your project, you'll still have the loops on your needles. Binding off is what we call removing the loops from the needle so that we can close up the project. Many patterns will instruct you to bind off in a pattern, which simply means that you'll follow the same pattern as the last row. For example, if you were doing a 1/1 ribbed pattern, then you would be binding off with alternating knit stitches and purl stitches. If you were binding off from a 2/2 ribbed pattern, then we would be alternating two knit stitches with two purl stitches. Keep this in mind going forward.

Let's pretend that we've just finished the last row of our project and we're now ready to bind off. How exactly do we pull this off?

First things first, we need to see what the first two stitches in the row are. If they're both knit stitches then we're going to knit stitch into them. Just make sure that you match the knit stitches and the purl stitches. With the first two stitches in the row out of the way, we're going to do something new. The two stitches are now on your right-hand needle. Take your left-hand needle and use it to lift up the first stitch on the right needle and pull it over the second and off the needle. Now your right-hand needle will have a single stitch on it, though it is the second stitch from the new row.

We're going to continue stitching the row, matching each stitch to the one it is going into. But as soon as we finish a new stitch, we'll use our left-hand needle to slip it over the first stitch and off the needle. So when we do the third stitch, we're going to be slipping off the first stitch so that the third stitch is all that is on the needle. When we do the fourth stitch we'll lift off the first stitch, which had been the third in the row, so that the only stitch remaining is the fourth in the row. Continue this until you finish the row. If done properly, then you'll have nothing on the left-hand needle but you'll still have a single stitch on the other needle.

At this point we're going to slip off that last stitch, grab our scissors and cut the yarn. We want to leave half a foot or so in length so that it will be easier to weave. It is always better to cut your working yarn too long than too short since we can always cut it again but we can't add more to it without a lot of extra work. We leave this tail to weave the ends, which we'll be discussing in just a second. But first we want to take the tail of yarn and slip it through the loop of the last stitch, making sure it is nice and tight. At this point we have successfully bound off the yarn.

We haven't finished the project yet, we still need to weave the ends. So let's do that next.

KNITTING FOR BEGINNERS

Weaving Ends

Weaving is an important part of knitting but it is one of the pieces which trip up beginners the most. We've spent all this time learning how to knit and then suddenly we need to learn how to weave, too?

Yup, we do. But don't worry, it's easier than you think. The first step is to make sure that you cut your working yarn with a tail of at least six inches. Don't worry if it isn't perfect, you don't need to grab the tape measure and check it. We just want to make sure that it is long enough to be weaved properly. You can use a yarn needle or a tapestry needle to work this weave, though I personally find the tapestry needle to be the easier of the two.

You can weave the tail into any part of your project but it is going to look weird if you don't plan it out ahead of time. You can always tell when someone didn't plan ahead because the weaved end is awkward and stands out. Picking a spot where it won't stand out is one of those skills that beginners will master with time and practice.

Weaving is incredibly easy and it can be done in so many ways that to give direct instructions wouldn't be useful. Rather what you are doing here is attaching the yarn tail to the tapestry needle and then pushing the needle in and out of the fabric, hence you are weaving it into place. We want to make sure that the ends of the yarn are hidden from the front of the project. We want to make sure that the tail is in a position where it won't catch and unravel.

But how about some tips and tricks that will help?

One popular way of hiding the yarn tail is to work the tapestry needle through the back of the piece, as this helps hide it. Working through the purl loops is an especially useful strategy. If you've been working an edge into your project, then you could hide the yarn tail vertically along the edge. Hiding along the edge is absolutely one of the most effective ways to hide the tail. If you don't have an edge to hide along then you could try using the seams. Don't worry, we'll be covering how to sew seams shortly.

Keep in mind that if you are working on a large pattern, one with multiple colors, then you are going to have many yarn tails which you need to hide. Don't wait until you finish the project to start to hide them or you're going to have a miserable experience and quickly find that the quality of the project sinks as it unravels.

Finally, give it time. Weaving the ends of a project together takes a lot of time, even when you're great at it and we're coming into this as beginners. Don't rush it and don't get defeated when it doesn't go the way you thought it was going to.

Sewing Seams

This is often the least fun part of any knitting project. It isn't that this is particularly difficult, really. It's just that it doesn't have much to do with knitting. The skill we use here is sewing, not knitting, so it can be quite annoying to switch into another skill set. Plus, since sewing the seams isn't as common in knitting as the actual knitting of stitches is, it is often one of the skills that knitters need a lot of time to develop. If you fast track your learning of this skill by deliberately practicing it, you won't feel so intimidated when it comes up in a project.

There are multiple ways to sew the seams of your projects together. We'll look at three of them in this section, so you can either practice them all or pick the one that suits you best. But first, why would we want to do this? For one, it is a great skill you need to finish up your projects. You can use the seam of your project to hide the weaved tail, so that's always a plus. It is also an incredibly versatile skill, especially for those that take on projects that require them to join different knitted pieces together. We'll first look at the mattress stitch, which is considered to be an invisible stitch. We'll follow this with a technique known as whipstitching and a quick look at the easy top stitch.

Mattress Stitch: We'll use our tapestry needle for each of these stitches. We can thread our needle using yarn straight from the ball but now would be a good time to use our tape measure to get a sense of how much yarn we'll need. To figure out this number, first align the pieces you are connecting together. If you are sewing the end of a project together, like you would with the edges of a pillow, then you can simply measure the edge. Once you have the measurement of how long you are going to need to sew, you can use your scissors to cut the yarn to length. However, we always want to have more yarn than what we measure, so take your measurement and cut three times as much yarn.

Tie the end of the yarn together using a slip knot. This will make sure that the end of the yarn doesn't get pulled through the project and undo all the sewing you're about to work on. We'll start sewing from the corner of the project. Many people start at the bottom corner, but you can work from top to bottom if you want. We'll push through either the left or the right piece first, starting from the back and coming out the front. Once you have worked the needle through the first piece, work it through the second piece at the same point in the project. If you worked it through the last stitch of the first row, then you'll work it through the first stitch of the first row in the second piece so that they mirror each other.

Move from the second piece back to the first piece, this time in a higher row. Come through the back again and then switch over and sew the equivalent space on the second piece again. Alternate between the two pieces in this fashion, always working a higher row when you return to the first piece. Don't worry about tightening the pieces together at this point. Instead, just focus on stitching them together in this manner. Then, after the stitching is done, we will pull on the yarn to tighten it up. This will bring the two pieces together nice and tight, though we don't want to make them overly tight. Pull them together firmly but gently.

If you are working on a piece that is more than a few inches long, we want to break this process down into smaller steps. Instead of sewing the whole thing together, sew three or four inches together and then pull it tight before continuing on. This will make the experience much easier for those large pieces since you'll be able to prevent them from bunching up, a problem that occurs when we pull our pieces together too tightly.

Finish up the seam by cutting the yarn, leaving an appropriately sized tail so you can weave it into the project.

Whipstitching: For this approach we hold the pieces we are connecting together but we make sure that they're backwards so that the fronts of the pieces are facing each other. Measure the size of the piece and then give yourself three times as much yarn.

With invisible stitching, we kept the pieces next to each other and worked through them one at a time. This time, we're holding the pieces together so we can push our needle through both of them at the same time. Once we've gotten the needle through both pieces, we whip the yarn back over them so that we can push it through them the same direction again. It is this act of creating a loop or of whipping the yarn that gives this technique its name. Keep whipstitching the pieces until you get to the end. If you are connecting these pieces together on multiple sides then this may be the point at which you want to rotate them so you can keep going.

If you are done with the connection, pull on the yarn to tighten up the pieces. Use your scissors to cut the yarn with a tail that you can weave into the project. If you've whip stitched the pieces properly, you should have no problem laying them down right-side out.

Top Stitch: With knit stitching, you can lay the pieces out by each other or hold them in your hand while you sew the seams. Laying them out will result in a seam without ridges but holding them will create ridges. Both these options are perfectly valid, it just depends on what the project you're working on is and which style you prefer.

Measure your yarn, cut it at three times the length. We start this stitch like we do the whipstitch, only this time around we won't be whipping the yarn back over the project. Instead what we're going to do is turn the needle around once it has been pushed entirely through the pieces and insert it from the opposite side. If we began by stitching right to left, our second stitch will be left to right. Continue along the edge you are sewing together, alternating the direction of the needle until you get to the end of the side. You've probably guessed it, now is a good time to pull on the yarn to tighten up the connection between the two pieces. Grab your scissors, cut the yarn and weave the tail into the project.

There you have it, three easy ways to sew the seams of your projects together. To practice them, knit yourself a few pieces using a simple garter stitch and then connect them together with a seam.

Fixing a Dropped Stitch

Dropping a stitch is what we call one of our stitches falling off the needle. It could fall off because of the way we were holding the needle or perhaps we had a poor grip or angle when we were transferring a stitch from left to right. For beginners, this can be a terrifying moment, one that plays out in slow-motion as the stitch drops off the needle. It can feel like the entire project has just come crashing down. But don't worry, fixing a dropped stitch is pretty easy. In fact, you might not even notice that you dropped a stitch until a few rows later. You can fix these too, though you'll want to have a crochet hook on hand.

How you fix a dropped stitch is going to be determined by whether or not it was a knit stitch or a purl stitch, so we'll look at both.

Knit Stitch: Picking up a stitch that has just dropped is pretty much the easiest thing in the world, so long as it hasn't run off. Just wait until you get to that stitch in the next row and stick it back on the needle.

If it's been a few rows since the stitch was dropped, then it'll be a little different. The first thing you need to do is figure out where the stitch was dropped. Once you know where it is, knit the round you're on up to the stitch before the dropped one. At this point pause and set down the knitting needles to grab out a crochet hook instead. When looking for a dropped stitch across several rows you can tell where it is supposed to be because the stitches to either side of the dropped one will be connected with only a strand of yarn that runs horizontally.

We use our crochet hook to catch onto these strands and then we pull them through the stitch that was dropped. We work our way with the crochet hook from the row at which it was dropped, up to the row above, then the row above that, all the way to the top. Working with knit stitches we want to stitch the crochet hook through the front of the dropped stitch so that we can catch it from the back. Having caught the yarn we then pull it out the front again. This repairs a row, so we then remove the crochet hook and pick up the knitting needle.

Once you have gone through all of the previous rows and get to the top row, you can use the crochet hook to slip the stitch back onto the left needle. Now when you use the right-hand needle again, you work your new stitch into the one you just repaired. When done properly, there will be no sign that a stitch had ever been dropped.

Purl Stitch: A purl stitch is the backside or the opposite of a knit stitch so we need to work it a little differently when we drop one. To fix a purl stitch we must first turn the project around, so that we're working from the back. Locate the dropped stitch and use your crochet hook, going from the front to the back. This is the front as determined by the side facing you, not the front side of the project itself. Use the hook to grab the strand from the dropped stitch and pull it through.

We are working with a purl stitch, so we want to make sure that the lowest stand is brought in front of the stitch that dropped so that it protrudes outwards. We then use our crochet hook to grab the dropped stitch and pull it through our loop. Next, we set our crochet hook down, or at least remove it from the dropped stitch, and then reposition the next strand up to create that protruding bump that is indicative of a purl stitch. This process is repeated until we've made our way back up to the row we're currently knitting, at which point we slip the stitch back onto the left needle.

There you have it, in no time at all you fixed a dropped stitch. I recommend practicing this skill on its own before you need to use it on a project. Knit together a four or five rows that are a dozen stitches long. Drop a stitch in the middle on the second or third row, then practice fixing it once you get to the fifth. You'll find that once you wrap your head around this skill, it is pretty easy to feel far more confident in your ability to fix a dropped stitch in your projects.

Fixing Holes

Holes can be a real pain in knitting. They are one of the issues that beginners face quite often. In fact, we're going to be talking about what causes these holes in chapter six. But for those of you not worried about "spoilers," holes are most often caused because the rows of your project are shrinking or growing thanks to added or lost stitches. That said, you might also create a hole by wrapping your yarn over the needle at the wrong point in the project, which results in more stitches than normal. There are many patterns in which we actually want to create holes and so if you are working on a project like that, you won't want to fix your holes. At least, not these holes. A hole can also form if you drop a stitch and don't go back to fix it.

Fixing holes is a lot more complicated than picking up a dropped stitch. Well, maybe difficult isn't the right word but it is certainly more time-consuming, frustrating and disheartening. The problem here is that, to fix a hole, you need to unknit the project back to and then past the hole. So, if your hole was a few rows back, you're going to find yourself undoing a lot of work. This approach can be demoralizing, but if you want to have a strong piece, you'll need to use it.

There is another option, of course, though it results in a project that is quite loose and it greatly reduces the quality of your work. I don't recommend this approach, but you may want to give it a try it regardless. In this second option, we continue working our project until we get to the problem stitch and then we drop it. This approach doesn't work if the hole was created thanks to a dropped stitch (but if it was, you can use the previous method to fix it much easier). If we created a hole by yarning over the needle at the wrong point, we have an extra stitch on our needle that we can drop and be good to go. The problem here is that there is now extra yarn in the project and the rest of the stitches are going to slacken because of this. This, in turn, reduces the quality and longevity of the piece we're making.

But, again, it must be mentioned that holes aren't necessarily a bad thing. A hole where you don't want it can be frustrating, but if it happens early in the project, perhaps you should consider working holes into the pattern. You can create holes on purpose by changing the gauge of your yarn or your needle. You might purposefully yarn over more often to create the effect. Just make sure that you take control of it and you can make a mistake seem like a design choice.

Of course, if you want to change between different gauges of yarn then you're going to need to understand how we do this in the middle of the project. This is the same way that we switch between colors, so let's turn our attention over to this technique before we close out on our terminology and abbreviations.

Changing Colors

Changing colors really isn't that hard. If it was, there wouldn't be so many amazing knitted creations with beautiful and intricate patterns of colors, striped sweaters and richly colored blankets. But thankfully switching colors is easy, so even beginners like us can master the skill quickly. Of course, you don't need to learn this technique if you don't like colorful knitted patterns. You can make plenty of great creations with block colors. But you would also be limited to using a single ball of yarn, since switching to a new one is the same as switching to a new color. If you want to master this craft, you're going to need this skill regardless of your thought on using multiple colors.

To change colors, we must first start with a color so we have something to change from. So, go through your normal process of tying a slip knot and casting on. Knit a few rows. This step isn't necessary but you will find that changing colors is easier when you have enough of a project to get a good look at. It will also be much easier to see the difference between the colors when you have a few rows to help them contrast each other.

When we work a pattern, we typically flip the project over at the end, so that we're stitching from the back. We do this so we don't need to whip our yarn back over to the opposite side. Instead, we can finish a row and then start the next row from exactly where we are.

Switching colors is always going to be easier to do when you're starting a new row, but it is a particularly good idea to do when beginning a right-facing row. That is to say any odd numbered row, so for this practice you should try switching colors for either the third or the fifth row. You can change colors at any time, of course, but sticking to these tips will give you the best looking project possible and we're always aiming for high quality when knitting.

Starting at the third or fifth row, drop your first color and cut the yarn from the ball with a six inch tail. We've just done what we normally do when we leave a tail on the back end of the project from where we cut the yarn when we've finished using it. But this time around we're not going to weave the end into the project. Instead, we're going to take the tail of our second color and tie it to the tail of the first color. We're tying together the end of one piece of yarn to the beginning of a new piece.

We now insert the needle into the first stitch just like we would do when starting a new row. We're going to stitch exactly as we normally would. You're going to find that your first stitch is going to look really bad, however. I'm saying it will look bad enough that you're going to think that you messed something up. It'll be loose and seem almost totally useless. This is perfectly fine and you should expect it whenever you switch colors between rows. Just keep stitching like you normally would until you've moved away from this first stitch a bit. Then you can tighten it up by tightening the last stitch on the previous row, as this is the stitch that your new color first pushed into. To tighten, simply just pull on the tails of the yarn. Not too hard, as we don't want it to be too tight.

After tightening, continue to stitch down the row until you come to the end. Work up to the next row and keep going. If you are sticking with this new color, then you can just keep going until the end. If you want to switch to a new color, you just need to repeat the method above. The new color may be the first color you used and, thus, not truly be "new," but we treat it as such and follow the same steps, unless we're working with short bursts of color that alternate back and forth. If this is the case then we can carry the yarn up the sides, which is to say we twist our colors together at the edge, skipping a row between each twist, so that the yarn travels up the side. When doing this, we don't want to cut the yarn from the ball, as we plan to continue using it in short order.

Carrying yarn this way is a lot harder than just switching between colors by cutting the yarn and tying the ends together. We need to be careful to work the yarn gently on the edges. We want it to be stiff, but we don't want it to be too tight. Basically, we want it to be smooth along the edges rather than digging into them. Switching between the colors again is as easy as dropping one color and picking up the carried one. We then knit the first stitch in the row, remembering that we shouldn't be surprised when it looks loose and low quality. We'll fix it once we're part-way through the row, just like we did before.

Finally, we come to the end of the project. We finish it off in whichever fashion best fits the project or our tastes. Of course, now we have multiple tails to weave. Plus we have those two tails that have been tied together. Regardless of which approach we used, we don't want these ends tied. So we untie them and weave the tails into the project. Make sure that you weave each tail, as you will have multiple tails thanks to using multiple strands of yarn.

Terminology and Abbreviations

There are many more terms that you will discover while exploring the world of knitting, especially if you work with patterns from other countries or decades. But the following terms should be enough to get you through terms mentioned in any beginner's patterns. Many (if not most) of the new terms you'll discover when your patterns increase in difficulty.

Alternate; Alt.: Depending on whether it means within a row or the row itself, alternating is to work a different pattern or stitch one after the other. Row one, three and five would be the same while row two, four and six would be different from row one but each the same as the others.

Beginning; Beg.: The beginning of the row.

Bind Off: To finish a project with a row that ties it all together.

Cast On: Adding stitches to the needle at the start of the project.

Continue; Cont.: Simply means to continue doing what you have been instructed to do.

Decrease; Dec.: Decreasing means that you are to make fewer stitches going forward, most often achieved through connecting stitches together or slipping a stitch.

Following; Follows; Foll. Folls.: Lets you know that the instruction comes after another one.

G. St.: Shorthand for garter stitch.

Increase; Inc.: To increase the amount of stitches you are working with, most often achieved by creating two stitches in the same place or by knitting two stitches at once.

Knit; K.: This may refer to the act of knitting itself, but it is most frequently used to refer to the knit stitch. The shorthand of K. will be followed by a number of patterns to refer to how many knit stitches you are supposed to make.

Make 1; m1.: This tells you that you will be adding extra stitches to the project.

M. St.: Shorthand for moss stitch.

Pattern; Patt.: In knitting, a pattern refers to the document or guide which tells you how to make a particular project.

Purl; P.: Along with the knit stitch, the purl stitch is the most commonly used stitch. The shorthand of P. will be followed with a number to refer to how many purl stitches to work into the project.

Pass Slipped Stitch Over; p.s.s.o.: The act of slipping a stitch and then knitting the next stitch. The freshly worked stitch is transferred to the right-hand needle. The slipped stitch is then moved off the right-hand needle while the fresh stitch is left on.

Repeat; Rep.: To repeat an instruction.

Reverse Shaping: This is what we call it when we work another side of a project from the one we started with.

Row: Knitting is done in rows. The bottom of each row is worked into the top of the previous row.

Slip; Sl.: To move a stitch from the left needle to the right needle without making a stitch. We do this to skip over stitches which we don't intend to work a fresh stitch into.

Stitch; St.: A stitch. It most often refers to a stitch that has already been made rather than one that is being worked currently.

St. St.: Shorthand for a stocking stitch.

Through the Back of the Loop; Tbl.: This refers to the direction that the right-hand needle is worked into the stitch. The purl stitch is done by slipping into the back of the loop.

Yarn Back; yb.: Moving the yarn from the front of the needles to the back of the needles.

Yarn Forward; yfwd.: Moving the yarn from behind the needles to the front of the needles.

Yarn Front; yf.: This tells us to leave the yarn in front of the needle rather than moving it to the back.

Yarn Round Needle; yrn.: The act of wrapping the yarn around the right-hand needle so that we can work a new stitch into a project.

KNITTING FOR BEGINNERS

Chapter Summary

- Binding off, sometimes called casting off, is the technique that we use to bring our project to an end. We get to the last row of the project and then we stitch the first two slots in the row. With these two stitches on the right-hand needle, we use our left-hand needle to slip the back stitch off the right. Continuing to knit the row, we always slip the back stitch off so that we end with a single stitch on the right-hand needle, which we slip off.

- Once we reach the end of a project, we need to use our trusty scissors to cut the working yarn. We should always leave a tail of yarn that is about six inches (sometimes longer is better, depending on the project). This is so we can weave the tail into the project.

- Weaving the tail into the project is done with our tapestry needle. Simply push into a stitch and then out another and continue threading the yarn tail through in this manner.

- There are many different ways to weave a yarn tail, but the important part is that the tail is hidden, so it is often best to consider where we'll weave it before we get to the end of the project.

- If you are working a project that will have the seams sewn then you should weave the tail into the seam to more easily hide it.

- If you are working on a project that uses many different yarns then you'll have many yarn tails to weave. Rather than leave them for the end of the project, you should weave and hide them as you work through the project.

- Sewing the seams of a project together is sometimes necessary, though many knitters find it annoying switching to a different skill set in order to finish their projects.

- There are three ways of sewing the seams that we've looked at: mattress stitches, whipstitching and top stitching.

- Mattress stitching is so named because the two pieces being sewn together are laid flat and the sides are stitched together from this position.

- We whipstitch a seam by holding the two pieces together, pushing the needle through them, and then whipping the needle and thread back over the project, so that our next insertion is from the same direction as the first.

- Top stitching looks like whipstitching, except instead of whipping the yarn back over the project, we make our second insertion with the needle going in the opposite direction of the first.

- Dropping a stitch is what we call when a stitch falls, or drops, off of our needle. If we catch it immediately, then we can easily fix it. If we haven't caught it in time, we're going to use a crochet hook to fix it.

- We fix a dropped stitch by stitching our way across our current row until we find the stitch we dropped. We then use a crochet hook to fix the mistake, starting at the row where it was dropped and working up a row at a time until we're back to the latest row. We can then continue knitting like normal.

- Holes can appear in our work if we've missed a stitch or if we've doubled up a stitch. Sometimes holes are an aesthetic choice and we may want them in our projects, but often they are mistakes. To fix a hole, our best bet is to unravel our stitches until we get to the problem stitch and redo it.

- Changing colors is a common technique in knitting. The easiest way to do so is to cut the first color yarn, tie on your second color to the tail and then continue. Other techniques include working two colors at the same time and twisting the inactive color up the side so you can use it later.

- There are a lot of terms and abbreviations used in knitting that can be hard for a beginner to follow. We looked at these in our glossary that you can return to whenever you need to.

In the next chapter, you will learn three knitting patterns for projects that are a fantastic learning opportunity for beginners. These will range from a washcloth (though one that is more difficult than you might expect) to a hat (which is also surprisingly complicated) and a floor pouf (which is shockingly simple, go figure!).

CHAPTER FIVE

KNITTING PROJECTS

Now that we've covered our two main stitches (knitting stitches and purl stitches) and how they can be arranged into intricate stitch patterns, as well as the essential techniques we need to finish up our projects, it's time to start working on those projects!

As has been previously mentioned, I recommend that beginners first practice their stitches to death before beginning a project. But, if you're impatient (like I am, honestly), then project #1 would also be a good place to start. However, the projects begin to increase in difficulty immediately afterwards and you'll find yourself needing to purchase more knitting needles and yarn thanks to the different sizes these projects use. I believe it is best to practice with whatever yarn you have on hard first and then to go out and purchase more depending on which projects you want to tackle. This way, you get plenty of experience before you start switching things up.

KNITTING FOR BEGINNERS

We're going to cover a handful of projects in this chapter, all of which are chosen to challenge you and help you practice new skills. Obviously, these projects are far from being the only ones out there. You can find tons of knitting patterns that range from blankets to scarves, gloves to socks and everything in between. If you aren't drawn to any of the patterns in this chapter then simply go out and find some patterns that you like. This is your skill and so you should use it as you feel is best.

Project #1: A Simple Washcloth

A washcloth is often one of the first projects that beginners take on. This is true whether we're talking about knitting, crochet or sewing. It's just an incredibly easy project for beginners, but one that can prove to be a lot of fun. Plus you get a new washcloth out of it and, if you're like me, then you can never have enough washcloths. You should be able to make two or even three cloths out of a medium sized ball of yarn.

Materials

For this project, you will need the following:

- Knitting needles (2), size 7.
- A tapestry needle.
- A ball of yarn, size 4.
- Your trusty scissors.

Instructions

To begin the project, first we need to attach our slip knot to our knitting needle. Next we need to cast on. This is a fairly small project but it is still going to require a few dozen stitches in each row, so cast on thirty-six times. Now comes the fun part. This project uses alternating knit and purl stitches for some of the rows, while it alternates the rows a bit as well. But just because it is a simple washcloth, don't think that it won't take you a good long while to knit. We're going to be working fifty-five rows before we cast off.

It would be madness to go over all fifty-five rows, so instead we're going to cover how to make the first half of the project. The second half simply reflects the first, so by learning half we'll be able to complete the whole. We're actually going to make it even easier by breaking it into sections. The first four rows will make up our first section. Rows five to twelve make up the second section. Rows thirteen to twenty make up the third and rows twenty-one to twenty-eight make up the fourth. From there we'll quickly look at how the pattern repeats so you can finish it on your own.

Rows 1-4: These rows use a simple alternating pattern. We begin with a knit stitch, then a purl stitch. Row one will follow this knit then purl pattern through to the end, which will end with a purl stitch if done correctly. We then flip the project over, so that we're working through the opposite side and we begin this row with a purl stitch, alternating between knit stitches and purl stitches until we come to the end of the row and finish with a knit stitch.

Observant readers might notice that these stitches are lining up this way. That's exactly what we want them to do. We're basically doing a 1/1 rib stitch for the first three rows. But row four throws a kink in the machine. When we finish row three, we're on a purl stitch. We start row four with a purl stitch and we use a knit stitch in the second slot. Here's where it changes. Use purl stitches for the rest of row four until you get to the last three spots. These last three spots will hold a knit stitch, a purl stitch and another knit stitch.

Rows 5-12: Row five is going to start our new pattern. We begin with a knit stitch, then a purl stitch, then another knit stitch. This gives us the first three spaces in the row, echoing the equivalent stitches of the fourth row. But here we begin our pattern. We use six purl stitches and then six knit stitches and then repeat this again. After the second repetition, we continue the pattern by using six purl stitches, but we find that this leaves us with only two spaces left. Use a knit stitch and then finish with a purl stitch before moving to the next row.

Row six begins with a purl stitch followed by a knit stitch. From there we use purl stitches through the entire row until we come to the last three spaces, which we fill with a knit stitch, a purl stitch and a knit stitch, thus making this row a reflection of the fourth one.

Row seven, row nine and row eleven are the exact same as row five. Row eight, ten and twelve repeat row four and six. In fact, going forward, we are going to see this be the case will every even row until we get to row 54, which is a repeat of row two.

So alternate between these two row designs until you get to row thirteen.

Rows 13-20: Row thirteen uses a pattern that is similar to the odd rows of the last section but this time the repeating pattern has been shifted over, so that we're purling where we knit and knitting where we purled. Start row thirteen with a knit stitch, then a purl stitch, then a knit stitch. This gives us the first three stitches in the row that serve as the border design for the washcloth. From there, we use six knit stitches followed by six purl stitches. Repeat this pattern and then follow the second set of purl stitches with six more knit stitches. At this point we come to the last three stitches in the row and we use a purl stitch, a knit stitch and a purl stitch.

Again, row 14, 16, 18 and 20 of this section are following that same pattern we previously established for even rows. That is to say, they start with a purl, then a knit, then purls all the way through to the last three spots at which point it goes into a knit stitch then a purl stitch then a knit stitch again.

This pattern repeats until you enter the next and final section that we'll look at.

Rows 21-28: This section follows the pattern of rows 5-12. So, rather than rewriting the same information here, just reread and recreate the pattern as previously explained.

From here we have reached the halfway point of the project but we have covered all of the necessary sections to finish it. Rows 29-36 recreates the pattern from rows 13-20. Rows 37-44 recreates the pattern from rows 21-28. Rows 45-52 follows the pattern of rows 13-20 again. Then the last three rows of the pattern repeats the first three rows.

All that is left is to bind off the project!

Project #2: A Simple Beanie

A hat is one of those projects, like washcloths, that beginners have a tendency to start with. After all, who doesn't like a nice warm hat during the colder months of the year? But despite the simple appearance of a nice beanie, this project helps you to practice many different skills. For one, we're going to have to work in a circle. We do this by joining the seams together. We're also going to use our tape measure to ensure that we get the right size, rather than relying only on a set number of stitches. That's not all, though. We're going to get a chance to practice decreasing between rows to bring the hat together at the end.

So this simple project includes a lot of skills. Plus, you may find that the only way to continue going forward at the end is to use your double-pointed needles, which is a great chance for beginners to start playing with new tools.

Materials

For this project, you will need the following:

- Knitting needles (2), circular, size 8.
- Knitting needles (4), double-pointed, size 8.
- A tapestry needle.
- A tape measure.
- A ball of yarn, size 4.
- Your trusty scissors.

Instructions

KNITTING FOR BEGINNERS

Begin with your slip knot and then cast eighty stitches onto your circular knitting needle. From here, we're going to begin knitting, however, we're going to do this a little differently from normal. For our first row we'll use a repeating pattern of one purl stitch followed by four knit stitches. We repeat this pattern of five stitches until we get to the end of the row. We're going to be using this as our basic design, since our goal is to have a rib effect throughout the piece.

But before we worry about ribbing or even the second row, we need to join together the start and the end of the hat. We do this by using one of our seam techniques from the previous chapter, though we want to ensure that we join together the first and the last stitch, not any of the others. This turns our row into a round, though we're mostly going to continue working on it in a row-like fashion and, thus, we'll stick with the terminology we've been using.

With the first row joined into a round, we're then going to use our tape measure to get our sizes right. We're going to measure out about ten centimeters and our goal is to bring the hat to this size in height by adding more rows. How many rows you add will be determined by the material you are using, so keep a close watch. These rows will use a repeating pattern of one purl stitch followed by four knit stitches. Keep adding rows until you've hit the proper height.

Once the previous step is done, we're going to switch over to a slightly different pattern. This following pattern is also going to be used according to the length we've measured, though this time we're looking to get to about twelve centimeters and so it should be just slightly longer than the previous section. The pattern we're repeating this time is the inverse of the last, one knit stitch followed by four purl stitches. When this is complete, you'll have a piece made up of two different rib patterns, with the second pattern going on just a bit longer than the first. This is going to make up the base of the hat. From here, we are going to begin numbering our rows, starting at one, as we need to bring the pattern together. To do this, we need to also begin decreasing the size of each row so that the hat naturally comes together at the top of the head.

For the first of these rows, we're going to use a repeating pattern from the first stitch through to the last. We start with a single knit stitch followed by a single purl stitch, then we purl two stitches together and end with a single purl stitch. So, this gives us a four stitch pattern that actually uses up five stitches. What do I mean by that? Well, we start with a knit stitch and a purl stitch and by this point you already understand how these work. But then we need to purl stitch together too. This means that we're going to make a single stitch but, instead of pushing through one stitch on the left-hand needle, we're going to push through two. So, what would have been the third and fourth stitch of the row is going to become a single stitch, the third. Then the fourth stitch in the row finishes with a purl and we start the pattern again. We had begun with eighty stitches but now we're removing one for each repetition. Since five goes into eighty sixteen times, we can calculate that we should have sixty-four stitches on our needle by the time we finish this row.

Row two and three are easy, as we don't want to decrease our size again so early. So we're back to a rib pattern. Start with a single knit stitch and follow it with three purl stitches, repeating the pattern through to the end of the second row and then continuing in the third row until the end.

Once we hit row four, we're going to want to decrease again. This time we're using a slightly different pattern from before. We had used a knit, purl, purl together and finished with a purl stitch pattern. But we've already decreased the size once by this point, and so we don't have as many stitches to work with. Because of this, our new pattern is now a knit stitch, a purl stitch and then purling together two stitches. The purling together of the stitches marks the end of the repetition pattern this time and some quick math tells us that we should end up with forty-eight stitches on our needles going forward.

Row five and row six are going to use a rib pattern like row two and row three did, only it has to be smaller now because there is less space. So for this rib pattern we use a knit stitch followed by two purl stitches and repeat it through until we get to row seven.

Row seven is going to decrease the project again but again we use a smaller pattern than before. At this point our repeating pattern is simply a knit stitch followed by purling together two stitches. So, we have three stitches being worked into a two stitch pattern. Since this will start to bring everything really tight together, you might want to break out the double-pointed needles at this part. Either way, you will have thirty-two stitches to work with going forward.

Row eight and row nine alternate a knit stitch with a purl stitch through.

On row ten we don't have any space left for a fancy repeating pattern. Instead, simply knit together two stitches and repeat this until the end. This should reduce the amount of stitches by half so that you have sixteen left.

Row eleven and row twelve don't even have enough space for a repeating pattern. Simply knit stitch each spot.

Row thirteen, our last row, is completely made up of knitting together two stitches, so that we drop down from sixteen stitches to eight.

At this point the hat is almost done, but not quite. Use your trusty scissors to cut the yarn but make sure you leave a long tail this time. Use your tapestry needle to thread the tail through the stitches. Normally, we don't like to pull too tightly on our stitches, as too much tension tends to be a bad thing. This time around go ahead and pull nice and tight on the tail after it has been threaded. Then weave it into the project and enjoy your new hat!

Project #3: A Floor Pouf

Were you surprised by how complicated it was to knit together a simple hat? I know I sure did the first time I tried! But this surprise goes both ways, as this project turned out to be far simpler than it looked. In fact, as far as bang-for-your-buck goes, this is one of the coolest projects you can take on. It's easy to pull off, looks great, is super comfortable, plus it makes for a great gift. Especially when you consider it's a gift that seems a thousand times more complicated (and expensive) than it really is!

Materials

For this project, you will need the following:

- Knitting needles (2), size 15.
- A tapestry needle.
- Two balls of yarn, size 6.
- A tape measure.
- A trash bag.
- Bean bag filler.
- Your trusty scissors.

Instructions

Begin your project with your slip knot and then cast thirty-five stitches onto your needles. This is another project in which you're going to want to continue knitting row after row after row until you get a rectangle that's roughly three feet long. You can always increase the size if you want. You can decrease it too, though I wouldn't recommend going below three feet.

For these stitches, you can just stick with knit stitches if you want, but I think that a 2/2 rib pattern is the most attractive. The key here is to stick with whatever pattern you decide on. You could use a plain pattern or a super complicated one, it is entirely up to you. The goal at this point is to simply make a rectangle of the appropriate size.

Once you have your rectangle, you're going to want to use your tapestry needle to sew the ends together. Next, pick which side of the pouf is going to be the bottom. With a new piece of thread in your tapestry, begin working from either the end or the beginning of the bottom row, threading the needle through every other stitch. This is another project in which we actually want to pull our thread tightly. A pouf doesn't need to hold onto its shape perfectly, but it does need to keep its insides in place and that means a tight seam is necessary. Once you've finished with the bottom, give it another look and see if you can spot any holes. These aren't necessarily holes in the stitching but rather just large gaps from where the stitches weren't very tight. Sew shut any holes you find.

The pouf should almost resemble a purse at this point. There is an opening at the top that you could use to store things in, if you wanted. We are going to fill it up but we're not going to be using it to store anything. Put your garbage bag inside with the top of the bag opening around the top of the pouf. Make sure that it is held in place as you fill it up with your bean bag filler. As you fill the bag, the pouf will also fill up, since the bag is inside of it. How much bean bag filler you use depends on the size of the pouf and how full you want it to be. I find that it is best to make it so that there is very little extra space in the pouf, just enough so that it shapes around your legs or head when you lay on it

Tie the garbage bag together when you have enough filler. Now take your tapestry needle again and close off the top of the pouf the same way you did the bottom. Look for any holes you can find and sew them shut so that the bean bag filler is more likely to be trapped inside. I say more likely because even though it is inside a garbage bag, it is one of those things that always seems to find its way out over time. If you find that your pouf begins to leak down the road, then you can open up the top by removing the seam. Replace the garbage bag and top off the filler as needed, then just sew it up again.

In the next chapter you will learn about the most common mistakes that beginners make when they first start knitting. By learning these mistakes you will be better prepared to avoid them or at least you'll know how to tackle them, should they arise in your work.

CHAPTER SIX

COMMON MISTAKES TO AVOID

Now that you've had a chance to go over all of the various stitches in the book and try your hand at the projects, let's briefly close out with a look at some of the common mistakes that beginners make. If you have been reading along closely, then you'll notice that we've talked about a few of these in passing. This is good because it means that people who started knitting before they got to this point can still benefit from this knowledge.

But for those of you who stuck around and who are reading this chapter before starting on any of the projects, congratulations. You are already demonstrating that you won't fall for one of the mistakes that beginners often make: rushing it. By taking your time to read about these mistakes before you get started you will be leveling up your knitting skills right out of the gate and making the experience of getting started knitting that much easier.

It is worth noting that mistakes aren't always bad. Yeah, sure, they can be extremely annoying and fixing them can eat up a lot of your time, but that doesn't mean that they're bad. When we make mistakes we are forced to learn hot to fix our mistakes and this learning process does a lot to increase our skills. So, while we're going to do our best to minimize the number of mistakes we make, let's try to view those that we do make as opportunities to learn and grow rather than just negative experiences that suck the value out of our work.

Stopping In the Middle of a Row

Technically, there is nothing wrong with stopping in the middle of a row. After all, so long as you use a needle cap you can easily keep all of your stitches on your needles. All you need to do is pick them back up at a later date and get started knitting again.

When you stop in the middle of a row and don't return to your project right away, a major question is left to be answered: which direction were you going? If you stopped in the middle of the row, you'll have some stitches on your left-hand needle and some on your right-hand needle. So which way should you go?

Honestly, there's no easy answer to this question. You're going to have to rack your brain and try to figure it out on your own. And that isn't very much fun, sorry to say.

But this mistake is easy to avoid. Simply make sure that you always finish the row you are on before you put your needles down. If you do this, then all of your stitches will be on the right-hand needle and you can simply start from where you left off by switching hands and starting the new row. This makes it easy to keep everything sorted so you can get back to knitting faster and with less of a headache.

Making Your Stitches Too Tight

Making your stitches too tight is one of those mistakes that beginners make often without realizing.

When you aren't sure exactly how tight your stitches are supposed to be, you can't really determine if you've made them too tight or too loose. It's hard to get your stitches just right at this point, but there are three common reasons why they end up being too tight, so if you avoid making these mistakes, you will be that much closer to having stitches with the proper tension.

The first issue is that you aren't making your stitches on the right part of your needle. Your knitting needles taper at the end to make it easier to poke them into a stitch but you shouldn't be using this part of the needle for the stitches themselves. You want to make your stitches on the thickest part of the knitting needle and then let it slip off afterwards. If you make your stitches on the tapered part then they're going to be a lot tighter than they're supposed to be.

Another issue you might have is that you are holding too tightly to your yarn and this causes the tension of the whole project to be off. This is another of those problems that can really mess up your project, but it is one of those things you need to figure out by knitting enough to get a sense of the right level of tension.

You might also be tugging on the yarn too hard after you make a stitch. You don't want to hold onto the yarn too tightly but rather let each stitch just sit as it is while you work the next one.

Growing or Shrinking the Size of Your Rows

This is a mistake so common that you'll even find experts making it. It's not that it is so much a beginner's mistake, but rather that it is a very easy mistake to make. If you're distracted for a moment, you could find yourself making this mistake. You're just going along, knitting your project together when suddenly you realize that your row either has too many or too few stitches in it. How does that even happen?

It's simple. You just knitted the first stitch twice or you missed a stitch at some point. It happens more often on the first and last stitch of a row. There are a few ways that we can fix this problem. We've already talked about what to do when we dropped a stitch in chapter four, so we won't go over that one again here despite the fact that it fits here as well.

If the size of your rows shifted because you've knitted the same stitch more than once, there are a few options that you could use to fix this problem. If the extra stitch is on a side of the project that you plan to seam later, you can simply decrease it once you notice it. Simply decrease at the appropriate part on the next row and then hide the extra stitch within the seam. If you catch it early, you can always unravel your yarn back to the increased stitch and do it over again. Finally, you could drop the extra stitch off your needle, unravel the stitch and just move the extra yarn into other stitches, though I consider this to be the worst option of the three.

Another way that your rows change sizes is through yarning over at the wrong point in the process. This creates a hole. You can find more information about fixing holes in chapter four.

Messy Knitting

Messy knitting is most often caused by either holding your working yarn too tightly or too loosely. The only way to get over this issue is to continue practicing until you have an innate sense of the right amount of tension.

Unfortunately, there is no real solution to this one except practice. We really should be practicing a lot. It isn't enough to just learn one or two types of stitch patterns and then be done with it. If you want to master this skill then you really need to practice!

Chapter Summary

- It is never a good idea to stop in the middle of a row. You can, if you need to, but it makes it easy to forget which direction you were going. It is best to stop when you finish a row.

- Making your stitches too tight results in a cheap looking project.

- The first and last stitch in a row have a tendency to be missed or double-stitched and this then increases or decreases the amount of stitches in the subsequent row.

- Messy knitting happens when you don't get the right amount of tension in your yarn. The only way to master this mistake is through practice.

FINAL WORDS

At this point, you are well on your way past being a beginner. In fact, if you have practiced all of the stitches in chapter three and the techniques in chapter four and tried your hand at individual projects in chapter five, then you've absolutely graduated from beginner to hobbyist!

Sure, a hobbyist might not be nearly as important sounding as master or expert, but the only thing preventing you from reaching that level is more practice. After all, we've already covered how we should always practice, practice, practice!

Before we turn our attention over to the question of where we should go from here, let's first take a brief look back at the journey that we've taken together. It's been quite a while since you started this book way back in the introduction. A quick refresher will help you wrap your head around the aspects of knitting that are the most exciting to you and, therefore, where you should be focusing your attention going forward.

In chapter one we looked at the history of knitting. This was a fascinating chapter in my opinion, because it showed the way that this creative practice traveled across the world and through time to end up as we know it today. We saw the way that interest in knitting vanished, then came back and then vanished again, only to come back even stronger because you can't keep a good needle down!

In chapter two we looked at the tools we use to knit. These included our needles, our yarn, scissors, tape measure, tapestry needles, stitch markers, stitch holders, row counters, needle gauges, yarn bobbins, yarn threaders, yarn guides and needle caps. This might seem like a lot of gear, but it is all quite inexpensive and it is actually a fraction of what you'll find yourself acquiring as you get more into knitting. After all, a crochet hook is incredibly useful for knitting since it lets you quickly fix a dropped stitch. One thing worth noting is that, while this book primarily looked at knitting with circular needles, chapter two introduced us to the other types of knitting needles that are frequently used. Getting more practice with these would be a great way to continue your learning.

Chapter three was a big one, but boy howdy was it ever jam packed with useful information! We began by first learning how to make a slip knot and cast on. This is the technique which we use to make the first row of stitches in any project. From there, we moved into the knit stitch and the purl stitch. These are the two stitches used in knitting and, through them, we are able to make dozens of other stitch patterns. In a way, they're basically the same stitch. The purl stitch is just the back of the knit stitch, after all. Having learned these two stitches, we then went on to use them to learn the stockinette stitch, the garter stitch, the 1/1 rib stitch, the 2/2 rib stitch, the 2/2 garter stitch rib, the broken rib stitch, the seed stitch, the moss stitch, the little granite stitch and the basket weave stitch. Once again, we covered lots of stitches, but this is one of the areas where there is just so much more that can be learned. It is a great place to look to for further training.

In chapter four we covered some essential techniques. You could easily argue that slip knots and casting on are essential techniques. But without learning those first, we couldn't have practiced the stitches of chapter three. So rather than stick all the essential techniques into chapter four, we covered some techniques we had left out of chapter three. These included binding off, weaving ends, sewing seams, fixing dropped stitches, fixing holes in our projects, changing the color of our yarn. We also looked at the terminology most commonly found in knitting patterns. Each of these skills can be done in different ways, which are another potential source of future learning,

In chapter five we made our own knitting projects, from a washcloth to a beanie and then a floor pouf. If there is an area in which I recommend more learning, it is with projects. By tackling new projects you increase your knitting skill, plus you get some cool new creations! What could be better than that?

We closed out the main-crux of the book with chapter six and a look at the mistakes that are commonly made by beginners. Since you just finished that chapter before getting here, I'll trust that you don't need a refresher yet.

I already suggested some areas where you can learn more about knitting, so what else can I suggest? Honestly, I would recommend looking for new projects. I would just find a project I like and then look at what I need to make it. If you need a new stitch you haven't used, you can google that stitch and practice it. Learn what you need to ask when you need new information. With the skills in this book, you have a solid base of knowledge that will help you easily learn more stitches and techniques, as the foundation of those techniques is already something you know well.

Another way I would recommend you practice is by redoing projects, such as the washcloth from chapter five, and seeing how you can personalize them. What if you made the washcloth using a basket weave stitch? How would that look?

As my parting shot, I say it is up to you to find out and try your hand at whatever arises your interest. You're going to have to get back out there and pick up another project and find out what makes you tick. Remember: it is all about practice, practice, practice, but also lots of fun!

KNITTING FOR BEGINNERS